Library & Media Ctr.
Carroll Community College
1601 Washington Rd.
Westminster, MD 21157

NEW DIRECTIONS FOR STUDENT SERVICES

John H. Schuh, *Iowa State University*
EDITOR-IN-CHIEF

Elizabeth J. Whitt, *University of Iowa*
ASSOCIATE EDITOR

# Student Affairs and External Relations

Mary Beth Snyder
*Oakland University*

EDITOR

WITHDRAWN

Number 100, Winter 2002

JOSSEY-BASS
San Francisco

STUDENT AFFAIRS AND EXTERNAL RELATIONS
*Mary Beth Snyder (ed.)*
New Directions for Student Services, no. 100
*John H. Schuh,* Editor-in-Chief
*Elizabeth J. Whitt,* Associate Editor

Copyright © 2002 Wiley Periodicals, Inc., A Wiley Company. All rights reserved. No part of this publication may be reproduced in any form or by any means, except as permitted under sections 107 and 108 of the 1976 United States Copyright Act, without either the prior written permission of the publisher or authorization through the Copyright Clearance Center, 222 Rosewood Drive, Danvers, MA 01923; (978) 750-8400; fax (978) 750-4470. The copyright notice appearing at the bottom of the first page of an article in this journal indicates the copyright holder's consent that copies may be made for personal or internal use, or for personal or internal use of specific clients, on the condition that the copier pay for copying beyond that permitted by law. This consent does not extend to other kinds of copying, such as copying for general distribution, for advertising or promotional purposes, for creating collective works, or for resale. Such permission requests and other permission inquiries should be addressed to the Permissions Department, c/o John Wiley & Sons, Inc., 111 River St., Hoboken, NJ 07030; (201) 748-8789, fax (201) 748-6326, e-mail: permreq@wiley.com.

Microfilm copies of issues and articles are available in 16mm and 35mm, as well as microfiche in 105mm, through University Microfilms Inc., 300 North Zeeb Road, Ann Arbor, Michigan 48106-1346.

ISSN 0164-7970          e-ISSN 1536-0695

NEW DIRECTIONS FOR STUDENT SERVICES is part of The Jossey-Bass Higher and Adult Education Series and is published quarterly by Wiley Subscription Services, Inc., A Wiley Company, at Jossey-Bass, 989 Market Street, San Francisco, California 94103-1741. Periodicals postage paid at San Francisco, California, and at additional mailing offices. Postmaster: Send address changes to New Directions for Student Services, Jossey-Bass, 989 Market Street, San Francisco, California 94103-1741.

*New Directions for Student Services* is indexed in College Student Personnel Abstracts and Contents Pages in Education.

SUBSCRIPTIONS cost $70.00 for individuals and $145.00 for institutions, agencies, and libraries. See ordering information page at end of book.

EDITORIAL CORRESPONDENCE should be sent to the Editor-in-Chief, John H. Schuh, N 243 Lagomarcino Hall, Iowa State University, Ames, Iowa 50011

Cover photograph by Wernher Krutein/PHOTOVAULT © 1990.

Jossey-Bass Web address: www.josseybass.com

Manufactured in the United States of America on acid-free recycled paper containing at least 20 percent postconsumer waste.

# Contents

# EDITOR'S NOTES

A university official visiting another campus for the first time would generally be correct in assuming its organizational structure was composed of four separate divisions: academic affairs, student life, business, and university advancement. This traditional administrative model has remained intact until recent times, as campus administrators have begun to apply certain corporate initiatives that are designed to decentralize decision making in organizations.

Even though such programs as total quality management (TQM) and process redesign are being adopted in the campus environment, it would be highly misleading to suggest that the old academic "silos" are gone. The best campus leaders these days try to create a work environment that acknowledges everyone's role in problem solving, program delivery, and the promotion of community relations. A good example of this recent attitudinal change can be seen in how external relations are handled on campus. Each major administrative unit—student, academic, and business affairs—is now being charged with nurturing important university constituencies in the interest of the institution as a whole. Community involvement, once the sole domain of university advancement offices, is as important to the success of a student affairs officer as it is to a development officer. Indeed, active and daily involvement with alumni, corporate partners, the media, state government, and other external constituent groups must be a strategic goal of every student affairs organization. Strong external collaborations inevitably enhance our base of advocates, our overall financial and academic health, and our perceived accountability.

Our challenge is to engage with our communities in ways that lead to constructive, not contentious, partnerships with external groups. The chapters in this volume seek to provide a general overview of the many and varied ways in which student affairs can forge strong partnerships with constituent groups. The authors suggest practical ways to connect with outside partners in order to improve the quality of student life, and also to deal with the changing nature of external relationships brought about by changing expectations of higher education institutions.

The book's title, *Student Affairs and External Relations,* suggests a broad number of issues. In the final analysis, the editor chose topics that she believed represent current challenges facing our profession (outsourcing, media relationships, assessment partners, and employer interactions), along with some less obvious but nonetheless important topics worthy of student affairs interest (state coordinating boards and external assessment assistance).

The first chapter is a general introduction to the changing role of external partnerships in student affairs work, with the author attributing much

NEW DIRECTIONS FOR STUDENT SERVICES, no. 100, Winter 2002   © Wiley Periodicals, Inc.

of the change to public expectations that universities and colleges deliver greater value for the resources provided to them. In Chapter Two, Russell P. Bumba Jr. writes about state coordinating boards and their relevance to student affairs professionals at both public and private institutions. Even readers who have no responsibility to public governmental boards will gain valuable insight from Russ's comprehensive look at the historical development of state oversight of higher education.

The next three chapters, on media relations, privatization of student services, and alumni partnerships, provide concrete suggestions on how student affairs staff might forge connections with three key constituents. Ted Montgomery and I remind us all that in the aftermath of recent tragic events that have impacted students it is exceedingly apparent that student affairs staff are as responsible as anyone on a campus for maintaining excellent media interactions. In Chapter Four, James Moore poses critical questions for student life professionals to ask when their campus is evaluating whether to outsource a student or administrative function. Tara Singer and Aaron Hughey describe several interesting programming opportunities designed to strengthen the link between students and alumni and that can benefit both parties.

Chapter Six highlights the evolving nature of our institutional partnerships with the corporate sector, especially those cultivated through the efforts of career services and placement offices. The author, Gary McGrath, discusses the many benefits that accrue to students and employers when these relationships are positive and enduring. Bonsall, Harris, and Marczak describe a student leadership development program that has been integrated into their surrounding campus community in Chapter Seven. And finally, in the last chapter, Marilee Bresciani presents an analysis of the extent to which student affairs currently uses external firms to assist in the assessment of student learning and development. She discusses where and when to seek outside help in measuring the success of student programs under review.

Mary Beth Snyder
Editor

*MARY BETH SNYDER is the vice president for student affairs at Oakland University in Michigan.*

**1**

*This chapter describes the evolution of student affairs over time and under varying forces of change and its capacity for creating collaborative partnerships as a means for improving higher education and serving students.*

# Student Affairs Collaborations and Partnerships

*G. Gary Grace*

An interest in partnerships has permeated higher education and especially student affairs circles in the last ten years. Recent growth of collaborative efforts and partnerships is a result of a variety of factors, including increased societal expectations for higher education and a genuine desire by institutions to be more responsive to external needs and conditions. The responses of colleges and universities to changing conditions have significant implications for student affairs professionals. Student affairs involvement in collaborative efforts and with partnerships can redefine the traditional role played by the profession, a role increasingly more vital to institutional priorities. This chapter traces the evolution of student affairs over time and under varying forces of change. In addition, it defines and explores the types, characteristics, and beneficiaries of collaborations and external partnerships.

## Student Affairs in the Face of Change: Evolving Roles and Responsibilities

The role of student affairs in a college or university is largely influenced by such internal factors as the distinctive character and traditions of the institution, its history, and its academic mission. Priorities of the governing board, the vision and goals of the chief executive officer, and the availability of resources influence the array of services and programs provided by student affairs. Other important factors that help to determine the responsibilities of student affairs staff include the needs and characteristics of the

NEW DIRECTIONS FOR STUDENT SERVICES, no. 100, Winter 2002 © Wiley Periodicals, Inc.

student body, the community in which the college or university is located, and the background and knowledge of the student affairs staff.

Yet numerous outside forces have always shaped this American institution as well. Economic, social, political, and technological forces have provided a constantly changing context in which colleges and universities must operate and respond. When colleges were first established in colonial times, institutions of higher education provided a religiously oriented liberal arts curriculum that catered to a select group of men destined to become clergy, magistrates, and political leaders (Brubacher and Rudy, 1997). The student affairs function, first performed by faculty and tutors in colonial times, contributed to the intellectual, religious, and moral development of students (National Association of Student Personnel Administrators [NASPA], 1989).

The burgeoning industrial demands of nineteenth-century America required a wider variety of educated leaders. Colleges and universities responded by preparing students for a broader range of roles and developing applied research efforts to serve the needs of a complex society. To meet these changing needs, new and varied types of institutions were founded, including publicly funded state universities, teacher's colleges, agricultural and mechanical institutes, and municipal and community colleges (Brubacher and Rudy, 1997). Expanding colleges and universities were more multifaceted than their colonial predecessors and required increased specialization of their teaching and administrative staffs. As the faculty role became more focused on scholarship and research, institutions appointed personnel deans to address student behavior and discipline (Fenske, 1980). Post-Civil War students sought stimulation in a variety of extracurricular activities, intercollegiate sports, Greek letter organizations, debate clubs, literary societies, and student publications (Brubacher and Rudy, 1997). In addition to their disciplinarian responsibilities, nineteenth-century student affairs professionals coordinated and advised the growing number of extracurricular organizations and services resulting from expanding enrollments, an increasingly more specialized faculty, and greater pressure by students for personal freedom (Rudolph, 1962). Adding to these traditional disciplinary and advising roles, student affairs enlarged after World War I to also include the personnel and guidance function that came into acceptance with the U.S. Army's use of testing and counseling during the war to better match strengths and aptitudes to military needs (Herr and Cramer, 1979).

The post-World War II and Vietnam War eras also bore witness to continuing evolution of the student affairs profession. "Student affairs was called upon to provide a wider array of services in the areas of admissions, registration and records, financial aid, housing, food services, student activities, personal and academic counseling, orientation, and special services to a growing student body" (Garland and Grace, 1993, p. 5). To better organize and deliver service as a result of this increasingly diverse and complex set of responsibilities, the student affairs profession embraced the use of student development theories and organizational change strategies as a means of enhancing individual student growth and of fostering an institutional environment that supported learning and involvement (Garland, 1985; Study Group on the Conditions of Excellence in American Higher Education, 1984; American College Personnel Association, 1994; Astin, 1977).

Trends that began in the late 1980s seemed to accelerate in the early 1990s. The pace of change and expectations for constructive institutional response pressed from all directions. A sobering sense that everything had changed permeated the academy, especially among student affairs staffs. The demographic shifts in age and diversity, increased costs of higher education and the resulting debt burden on students, declining state appropriations for higher education, the erosion of campus civility, problems of retention and graduation of various groups of students but especially students of color, the constant press for technological sophistication, and a perception of declining quality of graduates in the face of a highly competitive global economy placed intense pressure on institutions to provide leadership and responses to new societal demands (Levine and others, 1989; Hughes, 1992; Allen and Garb, 1993; Garland and Grace, 1993; Ausiello and Wells, 1997). In the minds of many, higher education was under fire and it was no longer acceptable to have "business as usual." As Charles Schroeder observed, colleges and universities were seeking ways to deal with overwhelming internal and external challenges and to improve student learning and undergraduate education (Schroeder, 1999, p. 5). Clearly, new strategies for changing institutions and student affairs staffs were needed.

## Need for Systematic Approaches to Organizational Change

External forces of change seemed to bring about campus crisis, but they also served up possible solutions. The idea of adopting management concepts and practices from the business world are not new to higher education. Since World War II, colleges and universities have experimented and adopted, with various degrees of success, a wide array of business practices—as means of holding staff accountable, ensuring cost-effective purchasing, establishing multiple levels of supervision, implementing checks and approvals, evaluating individual and personal performance, and conducting institutional planning (Sherr and Lozier, 1991). In a spirit of innovation and, at times, trial and error experimentation, institutions have looked for more encompassing systems of change and ones that heeded the advice of various critics "to leave the ivory tower and rub shoulders with the various stakeholders of higher education."

One such system of change that gained some attention in the late 1980s and early 1990s was that of total quality management (TQM). The concepts and tools of several TQM gurus such as Edwards Deming, Phillip Crosby, Joseph Juran, Masaaki Imai, Malcolm Baldridge, and others were often debated and frequently implemented in some form by institutions that desired change (Wolverton, 1994; Seymour, 1992). TQM approaches concentrated on such values as long-term thinking, shared vision, emphasis upon involvement and support of people, use of data in decision making, and continuous improvement of processes (Sherr and Lozier, 1991). This strategy of quality management seeks to improve the efficiency and effectiveness of the institution and to involve the campus constituencies in satisfying both internal and external stakeholders.

Heralded by many within the student affairs profession, TQM was not without its detractors (Garland and Grace, 1993). Despite strong advocacy of governing boards and the business community, and successes of some early adopters such as Oregon State University and Northwest Missouri State University, TQM did not gain widespread acceptance. The academy soon tired of the language and techniques of TQM, which appeared off-putting and foreign to many academics. Others observed that the necessary organizational culture and long-term view of change by leadership were not supportive of TQM principles at some colleges and universities (Leffel and others, 1991). In the final analysis, TQM requires serious commitment at all levels of the institution and patience for the time and effort necessary to achieve progress.

Because TQM philosophy insists on a climate in which there is no room for fear, use of continuous quality principles and processes did not appear to match the times and the call for major educational change. Strategic change experts identify three primary conditions for institutional change: (1) a major crisis, (2) outside pressure, and (3) farsighted leadership (Rosser and Penrod, 1991). Strategic planning as a system of organizational change was viewed in the 1990s and even today as a better fit for higher education than TQM. The most distinctive feature of strategic planning is its emphasis upon the external environment, a critical consideration in light of the enormous political and societal pressure for fundamental change in higher education as the new millennium drew near.

By the mid-1990s, other business sector change models with such names as "downsizing," "rightsizing," "restructuring," and "reengineering" were being explored by numerous colleges and universities. All such planning processes required an organization to identify the changes occurring within the environment, to assess its particular strengths and competencies, and to match the former with the latter in a plan for achieving future opportunities (Rowley, Lujan, and Dolence, 1997). Effective strategic planning involves scanning demographic, social, economic, technological, and political trends and then determining the likely impact those trends might have on an institution (Lozier, 1995). Such planning is typically focused broadly, either formally, informally, or both, and linked to critical and real issues confronting the institution.

Student affairs staff members are central to such institutional planning processes because of the very nature of the strategic issues facing higher education in the twenty-first century. According to Rowley, Lujan, and Dolence (1997):

- Who will our student be?
- What should we teach?
- How should we teach it?
- How will students learn?
- What are society's needs?
- How does society expect us to meet its needs?
- What role will learning play?
- How will we pay for it? [p. 11]

Given student affairs knowledge of and experience with enrollment management, developmental programming, student engagement in the learning environment, needs assessment and planning, and financial management, these strategic questions express familiar concerns. The answers to such questions form the basis of an agenda for constructive change for institutions and student affairs. Under such organizational change, student affairs professionals can provide a collaborative and creative role in the integration of student and institutional development as well as expertise and insight for moving the enterprise forward. The ultimate goal of such collaboration and cooperative planning is a comprehensive set of strategies— a flexible and realistic plan for the future—that integrates institutional initiatives and resources with societal needs and opportunities.

## External Forces at Play: Increased Interest in Collaboration and Partnerships

Closely aligned with the orientation toward the external environment is the increased use of collaborative efforts and partnerships. Strategic planning often reveals gaps, or what the Wingspread Group's study called the "mismatch between what society needs of higher education and what it is receiving" (1993, p. 2). For years colleges and universities have initiated or joined others in efforts to solve problems; improve and extend services; offer opportunities for community involvement, "town hall" meetings, and volunteering; motivate or heighten the awareness of different underserved population groups; restructure processes or linkages; conduct research; create networks; extend library or technological resources; provide professional development and preservice teacher education; offer mentoring, tutoring, internships, enrichment experiences, and career development activities; and share equipment, facilities, and personnel (Schroeder, 1999; Educational Partnership Study Group, 1996; and Garland and Grace, 1993). A new mind-set is required to first see and then to capitalize on coherent interrelatedness of on- and off-campus opportunities for learning, service, access, networking, and resource efficiencies. For student affairs, partnerships with the community, business and industry, government, cultural institutions, nonprofit and religious organizations, health and human services, and schools can create structured bridges for students with the world beyond the campus. In addition to extending service or leveraging limited resources, such collaborative partnerships enable student affairs to take advantage of external opportunities for student learning.

Educational partnerships appear to have sprung up and proliferated in recent years. However, as Garland (1985) has observed, collaboration and partnerships have been a part of our work for a long time: "For the last 100 years or so, colleges and universities have nurtured informal relationships with business and industry and vice versa. These relationships have recently become more frequent and more formal. They, too, have important implications for student affairs" (p. 53).

But what exactly is a collaboration or partnership? Simply stated, a partnership is based upon an understanding and agreement of two or more parties that they will work together on a given problem, task, or enterprise. Within student affairs there is a broad range of partnerships. Some have become vehicles for educational reform, and others have sought to improve student outcomes. Schroeder (2001) identified three primary types of partnerships in which student affairs typically engage: (1) collaborative partnerships with constituents internal to the institution, (2) partnerships with other educational sectors to the institution, and (3) partnerships with business groups, corporations, social service agencies, and municipal, state, and federal governments. An important subset of this latter category of partnerships often includes outsourcing and entrepreneurial arrangements as a means of securing sufficient resources for vital program, services, and facilities (Askew, 2001).

Sockett (1998, p. 77) describes four types of partnerships with increasing levels of complexity and necessity of trust:

Level I. *Service* relationship: Where an individual or unit volunteers/sells support for an institution-related function. Examples are bilingual outreach programs and university students performing in a community/school or volunteering physical labor and skill.

Level II. *Exchange* relationship: Where the parties exchange resources for their mutual benefit. Examples are faculty access to organizations for research and early admission of high school students to university programs from poor communities.

Level III. *Cooperative* relationship: Where the parties plan together and share responsibilities. Examples are membership of community advisory committees, grant-supported projects that end when funding is exhausted, and research on problems identified by communities.

Level IV. *Systematic and transformative* relationship: Where the parties share responsibility for planning, decision making, funding, operations, and evaluation of activities, and where each institution is transformed through the relationship. Examples are early identification programs and peer mediation projects.

Four studies, Sockett (1998), Rubin, Fleming, and Innes (1998), Baker (1993), and Tushnet (1993) have identified characteristics of successful collaborations and partnerships:

- Shared vision, expectations, and understandings
- Clearly defined and owned goals and responsibilities
- Focus on real problems
- A defined structure for making decisions among the partner institutions and those who represent those institutions
- A defined method for ensuring continuity among partnership personnel
- Measurable outputs by which to evaluate progress
- Capacity building—being able to do more collectively than individually
- Catalyst and growth effects—enabling other joint activities to be undertaken
- Sufficient time for institutional change
- Provision of financial resources and leveraged seed money to encourage ongoing funding
- Availability of professional development training for those whose roles and relationships will change

## True Beneficiaries of Partnerships: Our Institutions and Students

Students, our institutions, and society can benefit enormously from collaborative efforts. Sharing resources, people, technology, and expertise makes sense given economies of scale and the financially restrained environment higher education always seems to face. Academic enhancement through service learning, networking, community development, and out-of-class experiences can provide for a more robust learning environment. Joint curriculum development activities between academic and student affairs staffs provide many rich opportunities for students to enhance their education and to experience a seamless learning process. Partnerships between academic and student affairs provide opportunities for the information silos to be eradicated and the divisional missions to be better integrated.

Capacity is built through the creation of partnerships. As noted by Rubin, Fleming, and Innes (1998), "Social capital is the trust, along with personal and political relationships that allow communication and cooperation, and even make it an attractive way to work. Intellectual capital is the shared learning that partners build about what the other wants and needs and what will work for them, as well as a shared pool of knowledge about the problems and issues in the community. Political capital is the muscle necessary to turn communally arrived-at agreements into meaningful collective action (pp. 16–17)."

Successful partnerships create the essential social, intellectual, and political capital that can then be used to transform our colleges and universities into vibrant learning communities that attract students and produce graduates who desire to continually learn and create in the interrelated and connected world around them.

## References

Allen, K. E., and Garb, E. L. "Reinventing Student Affairs: Something Old and Something New." *NASPA Journal,* 1993, *30,* 93–100.

American College Personnel Association. *The Student Learning Imperative: Implications for Student Affairs.* Washington, D.C.: American Personnel Association, 1994.

Askew, P. E. "The University as a Source for Community and Academic Partnership." In L. H. Dietz and E. J. Enchelmayer (eds.), *Developing External Partnerships for Cost-Effective, Enhanced Service.* New Directions for Student Services, no. 96. San Francisco: Jossey-Bass, 2001.

Astin, A. W. *Four Critical Years.* San Francisco: Jossey-Bass, 1977.

Ausiello, K., and Wells, B. "Information Technology and Student Affairs Planning for the Twenty-First Century." In C. M. Engstrom and K. M. Kruger (eds.), *Using Technology to Promote Student Learning: Opportunities for Today and Tomorrow.* New Directions for Student Services, no. 78. San Francisco: Jossey-Bass, 1997.

Baker, L. M. "Promoting Success in Educational Partnerships Involving Technology." In *Proceedings of Selected Research and Development Presentations,* Convention of the Association for Educational Communications and Technology, Research and Theory Division, New Orleans, Jan. 13–17, 1993.

Brubacher, J. S., and Rudy, W. *Higher Education in Transition: A History of American Colleges and Universities* (4th ed.). New Brunswick, N.J.: Transaction, 1997.

Educational Partnership Study Group. *A Guide to Promising Practices in Educational Partnerships.* Washington, D.C.: U.S. Department of Education, Office of Educational Research and Improvement, Southwest Regional Laboratory, and the Institute for Educational Leadership, 1996.

Fenske, R. H. "Historical Foundations." In U. Delworth (ed.), *Student Services: A Handbook for the Profession.* San Francisco: Jossey-Bass, 1980.

Garland, P. H. *Serving More than Students: A Critical Need for College Student Personnel Services.* ASHE-ERIC Higher Education Report no. 7. Washington, D.C.: Association for the Study of Higher Education, 1985.

Garland, P. H., and Grace, T. W. *New Perspectives for Student Affairs Professionals: Evolving Realities, Responsibilities and Roles.* ASHE-ERIC Higher Education Report no. 7. Washington, D.C.: The George Washington University School of Education and Human Development, 1993.

Herr, E. L., and Cramer, S. H. *Career Guidance through the Life Span.* New York: Little, Brown, 1979.

Hughes, M. "Global Diversity and Student Development." In M. Terrell (ed.), *Diversity, Disunity and Campus Community,* Washington, D.C.: NASPA, 1992.

Leffel, L. G., and others. "Assessing the Leadership Culture of Virginia Tech." In L. A. Sherr and D. J. Teeter (eds.), *Total Quality Management in Higher Education.* New Directions for Institutional Research, no. 71. San Francisco: Jossey-Bass, 1991.

Levine, A., and others. *Shaping Higher Education's Future: Demographic Realities and Opportunities, 1990–2000.* San Francisco: Jossey-Bass, 1989.

Lozier, G. G. "What Is Strategic Planning?" In K. M. Alvino (ed.), *Strategic Planning.* Washington, D.C.: College and University Personnel Association, 1995.

National Association of Student Personnel Administrators. *Points of View*. Washington, D.C.: NASPA, 1989.

Rosser, J. M., and Penrod, J. I. "Strategic Planning and Management: A Methodology for Responsible Change." In J. F. Williams II (ed.), *Strategic Planning in Higher Education*. Binghamton, N.Y.: Haworth Press, 1991.

Rowley, D., Lujan, H. D., and Dolence, M. G. *Strategic Change in Colleges and Universities*. San Francisco: Jossey-Bass, 1997.

Rubin, V., Fleming, J. J., and Innes, J. "Evaluating Community Outreach Partnership Centers as Complex Systems: In Search of the 'COPC Effect.'" *Metropolitan Universities*, 1998, 8(4), 11–21.

Rudolph, F. *The American College and University*. New York: Vintage Books, 1962.

Schroeder, C. C. "Partnerships: An Imperative for Enhancing Student Learning and Institutional Effectiveness." In J. S. Schuh and E. J. Whitt (eds.), *Creating Successful Partnerships Between Academic and Student Affairs*. New Directions for Student Services, no. 87. San Francisco: Jossey-Bass, 1999.

Schroeder, C. C. "Collaboration and Partnerships." American College Personnel Association. [http://www.acpanche.edu/seniorscholars/trends/trends7.htm]. 2001.

Seymour, D. *On Q: Causing Quality in Higher Education*. New York: American Council on Education/Macmillan, 1992.

Sherr, L. A., and Lozier, G. G. "Total Quality Management in Higher Education." In L. A. Sherr and D. J. Teeter (eds.), *Total Quality Management in Higher Education*. New Directions for Institutional Research, no. 71. San Francisco: Jossey-Bass, 1991.

Sockett, H. "Levels of Partnership." *Metropolitan Universities*, 1998, 8, 75–82.

Study Group on the Conditions of Excellence in American Higher Education. *Involvement in Learning: Realizing the Potential of American Higher Education*. Washington, D.C.: National Institute of Education, 1984.

Tushnet, N. C. *A Guide to Developing Educational Partnerships*. Washington, D.C.: U.S. Department of Education, Office of Educational Research and Improvement, 1993.

Wingspread Group. *An American Imperative: Higher Expectations for Higher Education*. Racine, Wis.: Johnson Foundation, 1993.

Wolverton, M. *A New Alliance: Continuous Quality and Classroom Effectiveness*. ASHE-ERIC Higher Education Report no. 6. Washington, D.C.: The George Washington University, School of Education and Human Development, 1994.

*G. GARY GRACE serves as executive director and dean of the University Center of Lake County in Lincolnshire, Illinois. He has served as the chief student affairs officer at four colleges and universities, most recently as vice chancellor for student affairs at the University of Missouri–St. Louis.*

# 2

*State coordinating boards address a variety of issues that relate to students and to student affairs operations. In order to participate in shaping and addressing these issues, student affairs staff need to understand how these boards operate and how to work most effectively with them.*

# State Systems of Coordination: A Primer for Student Affairs

*Russell P. Bumba Jr.*

Throughout most of their history, public colleges and universities were autonomous. Perkins (1965) described this autonomy as the "doctrinal shield protecting the university from the state" (p. 8). This autonomy involved the right of trustees to govern colleges and universities free of outside controls (Corson, 1975, p. 51). Legally sanctioned charters, state constitutions, and state statutes designated certain areas of responsibility as the exclusive domain of the boards governing public colleges and universities. This domain included making decisions about the institution's mission, policies, programs, personnel, and the allocation of resources.

Since the inception of state structures for coordinating and governing higher education, that "doctrinal shield" has dropped and, in many ways, it has been significantly dented. Initially developed to ensure efficiency and to control institutional rivalries (Williams, 1980), today's coordinating structures address issues such as access, accountability, affordability, excellence, economic development, and responsiveness to state needs. Today's state structures for coordination and governance touch more than institutional governing boards and presidents, and their touch extends to all segments of higher education. The actions of these agencies and boards affect many of the areas that traditionally fall within the purview of student affairs professionals. Student affairs staff will need to understand how these state agencies and boards operate and, more important, know how they can most effectively work with these agencies.

There is no shortage of information about state coordination and governance of higher education. Numerous books, articles, research reports, and opinion pieces address this topic. However, it is not a topic that has appeared frequently in the corpus of student affairs' literature. It is a topic that needs to be addressed so that student affairs staff can better understand and appreciate the role they can play when state coordinating agencies are developing regulations and procedures relating to admission policies, merit scholarship programs, accountability, and equity issues. In addition, knowing more about state coordination and governance can help student affairs staff better understand issues that are important to governors and legislatures and understand the pressures and expectations placed upon their institutions' presidents and other senior officers.

Warren H. Fox (1995), while executive director of the California Postsecondary Education Commission, declared, "Statewide coordination may be the least understood and certainly the most under-appreciated component of the higher education delivery system." This chapter attempts to address this shortcoming by providing basic information about the statewide coordination of higher education and its development. In addition, this chapter identifies current and potential future issues that may affect systems of statewide coordination. Finally, the chapter offers suggestions about how student affairs staff can best operate within state systems of coordination.

## Statewide Coordination of Higher Education

McGuinness (1997, pp. 3, 7) used the term *statewide coordination* to describe the formal mechanisms employed by states to ensure that their colleges and universities are aligned with state priorities and serve the public's interests. He further stated that the overarching function of statewide coordination of higher education is to establish and maintain a constructive relationship between the state and postsecondary institutions. In the main, statewide coordinating boards and statewide governing boards serve as the formal mechanisms. Generally, statewide coordinating boards promote state-level postsecondary educational needs and coordinate the activities of individual or multicampus governing boards. Statewide governing boards differ somewhat in that they oversee the management of all colleges and universities. This oversight includes such responsibilities as developing and implementing policies, appointing institutional presidents, allocating resources among institutions, and establishing policies for student tuition and fees (*State Postsecondary Education Structures Sourcebook,* 1997, pp. 53, 54). For the purposes of this chapter, McGuinness' definition of statewide coordination will apply. Also, the terms *state coordinating agency* and *state coordinating board* will apply to both state coordinating and to state governing boards except when citing research that compares and contrasts these two mechanisms or reports on the number of states using either mechanism.

From the early days of statewide coordination, the specific form, structure, duties, and powers conferred to the coordinating agencies varied from state to state. Although a number of classification systems have been used in studies of state coordination, it is acknowledged generally that the complexities of state political, bureaucratic, and statutory arrangements make such classifications and comparisons among state systems quite difficult (Hearn and Griswold, 1997, p. 423).

Early classification attempts focused upon the extent of their authority and functions. Glenny (1985, p. 7) identified two broad categories of state coordinating agencies:

1. a single statewide governing board for all public colleges and universities
2. a coordinating board juxtaposed between the governor/legislature and the institutional boards that embraces all of higher education, public and private [p. 7].

Glenny (pp. 9–10) further categorized the types of coordinating agencies by distinguishing between regulatory and advisory boards and by defining planning/service agencies. Regulatory coordinating boards had the authority to approve academic programs, new centers, and new schools, and to regulate academic policies and discontinue instructional programs. Advisory coordinating boards only had authority to review and make recommendations regarding policy, programs, planning, and budgets.

Millett (1975) expanded this basic classification structure to include executive appointed agencies. Others (McGuinness, 1999, p. 197; Richardson, Bracco, Callan, and Finney, 1999, p. 3) referred to executive appointed agencies as planning agencies. These agencies existed in states without a statutory coordinating agency and had a voluntary convening and planning role primarily for the purpose of ensuring good communications among the colleges and universities.

Later classifications focused upon the manner in which postsecondary institutions are linked to each other and to the states. For example, in their examination of how state governance structures influence higher education priorities and the means for achieving those priorities, Bowen and others (1997) used the following taxonomy:

1. Federal systems have institutional and multicampus governing boards and a coordinating board with responsibility for all public two- and four-year institutions. The coordinating board also has "substantial authority for information management, budgeting, program planning, and articulation" (p. 1).
2. Unified systems have a single governing board that is responsible for all public degree-granting institutions.
3. Confederated systems have a planning or coordinating agency with some planning and advisory responsibilities and limited authority in the budget process. These systems also have two or more multicampus governing boards.

4.  Confederated institutions have systems with institutional or multi-campus governing boards and lack an agency with "meaningful responsibility for all higher education" (pp. 5–6).

During the early development of statewide coordination of higher education, the basic responsibilities assigned to these boards were similar. The Carnegie Commission (1971, p. 26) maintained that coordinating boards were established and superimposed over the institutional governing boards of public colleges and universities for the following reasons: (1) to avoid program duplication, (2) to use scarce resources more effectively, (3) to aid in the growth of postsecondary facilities, and (4) to assist in the development of state policies on the admission of students. However, the duties enumerated by the Carnegie Commission in 1971 do not adequately portray the responsibilities of today's state coordinating boards. McGuinness (1994, pp. 162–164) identified additional functions that states had assigned to their coordinating boards. These functions are (1) planning, (2) policy analysis and problem resolution, (3) mission definition, (4) academic program review, (5) budget development, funding formulas, and resource allocation, (6) program administration, (7) information, assessment, and accountability systems, and (8) institutional licensure and authorization.

State systems of coordination and state coordinating boards have undergone tremendous change throughout the twentieth century. Today the composition and structure of coordinating boards and their powers and responsibilities differ considerably from the coordinating boards of the first half of the century. A variety of historical, economic, social, and political forces contributed to the evolution and expansion of these state structures and their duties. The following section highlights some of the salient forces in the development of state coordinating boards and state systems of coordination.

## Historical Development

By the start of the twentieth century Michigan, Montana, Nevada, New York, and Wisconsin had already established state governing structures for higher education (Williams, 1980). By the start of World War II, ten additional states established statewide governing boards, and one state, Oklahoma, established the first statewide coordinating board (Richardson, Bracco, Callan, and Finney, 1999, p. 5). By 1997 all of the states had established a board or agency that exercised statewide postsecondary functions. Twenty-one states had governing boards, twenty-six had coordinating boards, and three had planning agencies (*State Postsecondary Education Structures Sourcebook,* 1997, pp. 133–152).

Over the years states established these structures because of needs and objectives important at the time and because of circumstances unique to a state (McGuinness, 1997, p. 20). This section presents information about the needs, objectives, and circumstances affecting the development of statewide coordination between 1900 and the end of World War II, between 1945 and 1990, and from 1990 until the end of the twentieth century.

**1900 to 1945.** Williams' (1980) presentation at an annual meeting of the Association for the Study of Higher Education highlighted how state needs, state objectives, and state-specific circumstances contributed to the development, growth, and evolution of state coordination throughout this period. Acknowledging that government officials and business leaders exerted pressures upon institutions of higher education to become more efficient, Williams posited that the rapid acceleration toward state coordination and governance taking place between 1905 and 1945 could, in large part, be attributed to a single problem area: "the rivalry between competing public colleges and universities within state borders." This rivalry resulted in wastefulness, unnecessary duplication of academic programs, and calls for legislators and state officials to intercede on behalf of certain colleges and universities. To address these problems, several states solicited assistance from the U.S. Bureau of Education. The results of studies conducted by this bureau motivated and directed the establishment of statewide coordinating and governing boards. A study in the state of Washington conducted by the bureau under the direction of Samuel Capen (1916) provides a useful example.

State officials requested the study because of problems between the "University in Seattle and the State College in Pullman," and also requested the study team to report on the work of the normal schools. Capen's team noted the need for officials from the state's public institutions to meet together in order to better coordinate their work and academic programs. The study team suggested further that this centralized coordinating structure could "study state educational problems in a nonpartisan spirit for the purpose of determining what is and what is not needed and that it can bring state institutions to comply with its conclusions" (p. 61).

Challenges facing higher education after the end of the Second World War raised doubt about the ability of the coordinating boards to address these problems in a non-partisan manner and raised doubts about state institutions voluntarily complying with the boards' decisions.

**1945 to 1990.** During the post-World War II era a variety of factors profoundly changed higher education in the United States and the relationship between institutions of higher education and state governments. The influx of veterans taking advantage of the GI Bill greatly increased the demand for higher education. Years later this demand grew greater as a result of the "baby boomers" (Richardson, Bracco, Callan, and Finney, 1999, p. 6). Not only did this period produce an increase in the number of students but colleges and universities grew in complexity, the number of postsecondary institutions and campuses increased, and the amount of state funding for higher education increased considerably. In addition, higher education's growth and increased complexity spurred increased political infighting for resources and increased institutional lobbying efforts (Hearn and Griswold, 1997, p. 421). These conditions created fertile ground for the rapid growth in the number of states employing systems of coordination. Glenny (1985, p. 1) asserted that state lawmakers looked to state coordination as a response to unseemly competition among colleges and universities for funds, for new programs, for new facilities, and for students. He viewed coordination as the means "to bring order to the inevitable chaos of institutional parochialism in pursuing self-interests" (p. 1). In 1950, sixteen states had some form of statewide coordination.

Two postwar actions by the federal government significantly contributed to the development of statewide coordination. The Higher Education Facilities Act of 1963 required any state seeking to use federal funds for new campus construction to establish or designate a state facilities commission on which representatives from public and private colleges and universities were to serve (Berdahl and MacTaggart, 1999, p. 3).

The 1972 Higher Education Amendments affected the development of state coordination in three ways. First, the amendments modified eligibility for federal student financial aid programs by broadening the range of institutions encompassed under the term *postsecondary education*. This change depended on state licensure of postsecondary institutions, and this requirement expanded the oversight responsibilities of state governments. Many states delegated this responsibility to coordinating boards. Second, the federal State Student Incentive Grant program was established. This program provided matching funds to states for need-based aid programs. Many existing coordinating boards took on responsibility for student aid administration. Third, section 1202 of the 1972 Higher Education Amendments linked state eligibility for certain federal funds to the establishment or designation of statewide planning commissions, called 1202 commissions. These planning commissions would serve as a means to ensure the effective and efficient use of all resources—federal, state, and private (McGuinness, 1997, p. 21; Richardson, Bracco, Callan, and Finney, 1999, p. 8). In addition, Section 1202 mandated that the state commission be "broadly and equitably representative of the general public and of public, private, and proprietary institutions of postsecondary education."

By the mid-1970s forty-seven states had some form of statewide coordination (McGuinness, 1994). Callan (1991) asserted that during the post-World War II era the primary missions of state coordinating boards were to promote the orderly growth of higher education and to insulate decisions regarding growth from parochial and political interests. By the early 1970s the basic pattern of statewide coordination was in place. The state coordinating boards developed master plans, set parameters for program growth, engaged in program review and approval, implemented funding formulas, developed capital expenditure priorities, and operated grant and loan programs (Mingle, 1997, p. 411). However, from the mid-1970s throughout the

1980s new issues and challenges confronted the states and their postsecondary institutions. These issues and challenges included much more than facing decreasing enrollments and shrinking state appropriations for higher education. Issues relating to academic quality and institutional accountability began to appear on the agendas of governors and state legislators. Mandates requiring measurable outcomes for higher education and examinations of the effectiveness of postsecondary institutions began springing up nationwide (Epper and Russell, 1996, p. 4). In addition to these mandates, governors also sought to connect postsecondary education to the states' social and economic agendas (McGuinness, 1997, p. 22). Governors and legislators expected coordinating boards to become change agents, to affect the overall direction of the state postsecondary system, and to provide incentives for colleges and universities for the improvement of internal quality and efficiency (Ewell, 1985, pp. 8–11; McGuinness, 1997, p. 23).

From 1975 until the end of the 1980s thirty states amended the structures and/or the responsibilities of their state coordinating agencies (*State Postsecondary Education Structures Sourcebook*, 1997, pp. 133–154). Some of the changes came about because governors and legislators questioned the extent to which state systems of coordination, designed for earlier periods, could meet the demands facing higher education near the end of the century. The questions prompted assessments and research to determine the effectiveness and appropriateness of the state structures and to provide information that could direct changes.

**1990 to 2000.** T. Edward Hollander (1994b), in an address made at the 41st Annual Meeting of the State Higher Education Executive Officers, offered high praise for the effectiveness of state coordinating boards during the period of rapid growth in the 1970s and for the ability of these boards to successfully shift the agenda to the issues of quality and expanded access in the 1980s.

While Hollander and others had high praise for the effectiveness of state coordinating boards, not all agreed with his view. The first half of the 1990s saw these coordinating agencies questioned. James L. Fisher's (1995) opinion piece in *The Chronicle of Higher Education* exemplified the disagreements and generated considerable debate. He argued that statewide coordination failed to bring about more efficient operations, failed to improve academic programs, and stifled institutional governance.

Hollander (1994a), former chancellor of the New Jersey Department of Higher Education, predicted that the attacks on coordinating boards could "touch off a national debate on their effectiveness as advocates of higher education, guarantors of quality, and guardians of institutional autonomy." The latter half of the 1990s demonstrated the accuracy of Hollander's prediction. One of the biggest changes occurred in New Jersey and involved the New Jersey Department of Higher Education.

In 1994 the New Jersey Legislature approved the Higher Education Restructuring Act. The act dissolved the State Board of Higher Education and the Department of Higher Education and established a tripartite model composed of institutional governing boards, a Presidents' Council, and a Commission on Higher Education. The institutional governing boards became responsible for planning, policy development, tuition and fees, academic programs, degree requirements, and submitting a budget request to the state. The responsibilities of the Presidents' Council included new program review, the formation of new regional and cooperative programs, policies relating to transfer and articulation, and policy recommendations to the governor and legislature. The Commission on Higher Education's responsibilities included systemwide coordination, research, planning, and advocacy ("The Five-Year Assessment of Higher Education Restructuring," 1999, pp. 1–2).

New Jersey's Higher Education Restructuring Act was built on the assumption that the elimination of unnecessary state oversight would better enable the colleges and universities to fulfill their missions, respond to state needs, and provide an affordable and accessible system of higher education. The act also mandated that the Presidents' Council and Commission on Higher Education conduct a comprehensive review of the new structure and submit a report to the state legislature before July 1, 1999. This report acknowledged that some operational areas needed attention; however, it also acknowledged that the new structure "spurred institutional autonomy, collaboration, and innovation within a coordinated higher education system" ("The Five-Year Assessment of Higher Education Restructuring," 1999, p. 12).

In addition to New Jersey, other states reexamined their coordinating structures as governors and state legislatures sought ways to improve the responsiveness and performance of their states' postsecondary systems. Some of the reexaminations resulted in changes that strengthened the authority of existing coordinating boards, and some resulted in boards being replaced with another type of structure (McGuinness, 1997, p. 26). The Southern Regional Education Board, in its 1995 Legislative Briefing (1995), reported on the restructuring of South Carolina's Commission on Higher Education. The restructured commission reduced the membership and changed the composition to provide for more institutional representation. In its 1997 Legislative Briefing, the Southern Regional Education Board reported on the actions taken in Louisiana to strengthen the role of its Board of Regents, in Arkansas to abolish its State Board of Higher Education and replace it with the Arkansas Higher Education Coordinating Board, and in Kentucky to replace its Council on Higher Education with the Council on Postsecondary Education.

Does type of structure matter? A comparative study conducted by Bowen and others (1997) examined how state governance structures influenced higher education priorities and the means for achieving those priorities. The analysts reported a strong link between governance structure and the performance of higher education systems. Federal and unified systems had the capacity to better identify priorities and to shape institutional responses through information management, budgeting, program planning, and articulation (p. 1).

Some changes came about because of state legislative mandates to assess the effectiveness of the state systems. For example, Colorado's House Bill 99–1289 directed the Department of Higher Education to study the performance of higher education in the state and determine whether any changes or improvements were needed to more effectively serve the citizens of the state. The bill also called for an examination of the Colorado Commission on Higher Education ("Steady Progress: Higher Education Governance in Colorado at the Dawn of the 21st Century," 2000, p. 3).

The National Center for Postsecondary Improvement undertook a multistage research project designed, in part, to assess the extent to which state systems of higher education had implemented assessment policies and practices and to measure state progress toward this end. The first phase of the project focused upon describing each state's assessment policies and practices, to note emergent themes, and to establish a foundation for the later stages of the research project (Nettles, Cole, and Sharp, 1997, p. 3). The analysis of state documents demonstrated that two states, New Jersey and Texas, initiated state assessment initiatives in the late 1970s, that most of the states had assessment initiatives by the end of the 1980s, that 20 percent of the states passed assessment initiatives in the 1990s, and that four states did not have any assessment initiatives at the time of the initial stage of the study (Nettles, Cole, and Sharp, 1997, p. 30).

In general, today's state coordinating boards have broadened responsibilities that include an interest in measuring outcomes and enhancing academic quality in higher education and in connecting postsecondary education to the states' social and economic agendas. A number of historical, economic, social, and political forces contributed to the evolution and expansion of these state structures and their duties. Current trends and future issues will result in further changes. Perspectives about some of these issues and trends can be gleaned from the governors and the chief executive officers of state coordinating agencies.

## Current Trends and Future Issues

The National Governors Association's Center for Best Practices [http://www.nga.org/center/topics], noting that higher education presents today's governors with unparalleled opportunities and unique challenges, reported that the association established a four-year project, jointly led by two governors, on the future of higher education. This project will identify potential state policies that will respond to the following challenges: (1) managing a higher education environment that has become more varied and competitive because of distance learning, (2) closing the gap in educational attainment between whites and minority groups, (3) funding postsecondary institutions on the basis of outcomes and quality rather than reputation, and (4) finding more cost-effective ways to provide higher education.

Many governors have provided additional information about future issues and trends deemed important in their states. Markowitz, Brower, and Reindl (2000) gathered information about future trends important to governors through a review of the state of the state messages given by governors in forty-three states during the first three months of 1999. The researchers reported that the messages shared considerable common ground in the following areas that directly and indirectly affect higher education: (1) teaching and learning, (2) higher education's role in the new economy, (3) access and seamlessness in higher education, and (4) financing and affordability of higher education.

Russell (2000) reported the results of a State Higher Education Executive Officers Association's survey of the chief executive officers of statewide coordinating boards and governing boards. This survey solicited opinions about the importance of various issues confronting higher education in their states and information about changing priorities in the state. The top five issues, in priority order, follow: (1) teacher preparation and professional development, (2) workforce preparation, (3) effectiveness and accountability, (4) K–16 systems-linkages between K–12 and postsecondary education, and (5) instructional technology and distance learning. Perhaps instructional technology will provide the greatest stimulus for change. Boundaries play a very important role in state systems and boundaries become meaningless in a distance learning environment. Also, distance learning will present interesting challenges for state coordinating agencies as they deal with responsibilities relating to program approval and review. Mingle and Epper (1997, p. 482) predicted that these types of issues would create a new context in which these boards must operate. They envisioned that these boards will shift their focus from regulating and planning to creating opportunities, and from institutions to students. Because of this shifting focus and because of the functions and responsibilities currently assigned to coordinating boards, student affairs staff should have opportunities to work with these state structures and have opportunities to provide input as policies and regulations are being considered and developed. In order to work effectively with state coordinating boards and their staff, student affairs staff will need to know about their state's board and how to communicate with it and its staff members.

## Student Affairs

In order to work effectively with these organizations, student affairs staff must know the structure, functions, organization, and responsibilities of their state system of coordination. Much of this information can be obtained by reading the enabling legislation that established the state system and related amendments. In addition, student affairs staff should review their state coordinating agency's agenda and minutes, as well as reports, planning documents, and other publications produced by the state coordinating agency. This review will help in the identification of issues, proposals, and projects that might affect student affairs operations.

In addition to information available at the state agency's and the state government's web sites, useful information and reports can be obtained from the web sites of various organizations and professional associations. Three suggested sites follow:

- *The National Governors Association [http://www.nga.org]*. This organization provides support and research assistance to governors and their senior staff. The research assistance includes briefing papers on a wide range of issues affecting state governments. The association's best practices center provides technical assistance, information, and policy analysis on state educational policy issues.
- *State Higher Education Executive Officers [http://www.sheeo.org]*. This association assists its members, the chief executive officers of state coordinating and governing boards, by providing professional development opportunities, by serving as a liaison between the states and the federal government, by studying higher education policy issues and publishing reports, and by implementing projects to enhance the capacity of the SHEEO agencies to improve higher education.
- *The Education Commission of the States [http://www.ecs.org]*. This is a state membership organization that provides background information on coordination and governance to policy makers and assists states in designing and implementing new structures. This organization also produces occasional papers and reports that address issues of higher education governance, and it has regularly produced sourcebooks that provide information about the structure, responsibilities, and membership of state coordinating and governing boards.

Knowing the issues a state agency plans to address or programs it plans to implement may spur an interest in contacting agency staff and providing opinions and observations about the potential impact upon students or a student affairs operation. Knowing the agency's structure provides only a partial foundation for effective communications. To complete the foundation, student affairs staff need to know how their college or university prefers to communicate with the state agency and act according to the institution's procedures.

There may be times when the state agency will solicit information from student affairs staff. Given the agency's interest in issues relating to accountability and institutional effectiveness, student affairs staff may be asked, by the state agency or by the institution's president, to provide assessment information about programs and services. When providing information to the state coordinating agency, remember the target audience, prepare the report accordingly, and avoid two common problems. One is best described by the acronym DRIP (data rich, information poor) (Becker, Huselid, and Ulrich, 2001). When responding to requests for information, don't emphasize the data collected through your assessment. Instead, highlight the findings and describe, in jargon-free language, why they are important. The second problem involves highlighting the findings. In place of thick, rich descriptions, use brief descriptive statements. If any additional information is needed, you will most likely be asked to provide it.

## Conclusion

State coordinating boards have moved from regulatory roles to larger state policy roles (Russell, 2000). As a result of this shift, today's boards address a variety of issues that relate to students and to student affairs operations. Student affairs staff have opportunities to participate in shaping and addressing these issues. Knowing the coordinating board's structure and responsibilities, knowing the state's political landscape and agenda for higher education, and knowing how your college communicates with this agency are basic components in establishing an effective working relationship with state coordinating agencies.

## References

Becker, B. E., Huselid, M. A., and Ulrich, D. *The HR Scorecard: Linking People, Strategy, and Performance.* Cambridge, Mass.: Harvard Business School Press, 2001.

Berdahl, R. O. (ed.). *Evaluating Statewide Boards.* New Directions for Institutional Research, no. 2. San Francisco: Jossey-Bass, 1975.

Berdahl, R. O., and MacTaggart, T. J. *Charter Colleges: Balancing Freedom and Accountability, White Paper No. 10.* Boston: Pioneer Institute for Public Policy Research, 1999.

Bowen, F. M., and others. "State Structures for the Governance of Higher Education: A Comparative Study." Research paper prepared for State Structures for the Governance of Higher Education and the California Higher Education Policy Center, Spring 1997.

Callan, P. M. "Perspectives on the Current Status and the Emerging Policy Issues for State Coordinating Boards," Association of Governing Boards Occasional Paper, No. 2. Washington, D.C.: Association of Governing Boards, 1991.

Capen, S. P. "Recent Movements in College and University Administration." U.S. Department of the Interior, Bureau of Education, Bulletin, 1916 (46), p. 61.

Carnegie Commission. *The Capitol and the Campus: State Responsibility for Post-Secondary Education.* New York: McGraw-Hill, 1971.

Corson, J. J. *The Governance of Colleges and Universities.* New York: McGraw-Hill, 1975.

Epper, R. M., and Russell, A. B. *Trends in State Coordination and Governance: Historical and Current Perspectives.* Denver: State Higher Education Executive Officers, 1996.

Ewell, P. T. *Levers for Change: The Role of State Government in Improving the Quality of Postsecondary Education.* Denver: Education Commission of the States, 1985.

Fisher, J. L. "The Failure of Statewide Coordination." *Chronicle of Higher Education,* June 16, 1995, p. A48.

"The Five-Year Assessment of Higher Education Restructuring: A Joint Report of the New Jersey Commission on Higher Education and the New Jersey Presidents' Council," Trenton, N.J., June 25, 1999.

Fox, W. "Letter to the Editor." *Chronicle of Higher Education,* July 14, 1995.

Glenny, L. A. *State Coordination of Higher Education: The Modern Concept.* Denver: State Higher Education Executive Officers, 1985.

Hearn, J. C., and Griswold, C. P. "State-Level Centralization and Policy Policy Innovation in U.S. Postsecondary Education." In L. F. Goodchild, C. D. Lovell, E. R. Hines, and J. I. Gill (eds), *Public Policy and Higher Education.* Needham Heights, Mass.: Pearson Custom Publishing, 1997.

Hollander, T. E. "Coordinating Boards Under Attack." *Trusteeship,* July–Aug. 1994a, pp. 17–19.

Hollander, T. E. "Board Effectiveness: What Is It?" Paper presented at the 41st annual meeting of the State Higher Education Executive Officers, Hilton Head, S.C., August 1, 1994b.

Markowitz, M., Brower, D., and Reindl, T. *State Issues Digest.* Washington, D.C.: American Association of State Colleges and Universities, 2000.

McGuinness, A. C., Jr. "The States and Higher Education." In P. G. Altbach, R. O. Berdahl, and P. J. Gumport (eds.), *Higher Education in American Society, Third Edition.* Amherst, N.Y.: Prometheus, 1994.

McGuinness, A. C., Jr. "Essay: The Functions and Evolution of State Coordination and Governance in Postsecondary Education," *State Postsecondary Education Structures Sourcebook.* Denver: Education Commission of the States, 1997, pp. 1–45.

McGuinness, A. C., Jr. "The States and Higher Education." In P. G. Altbach, R. O. Berdahl, and P. J. Gumport (eds.), *American Higher Education in the Twenty-First Century.* Baltimore: Johns Hopkins University Press, 1999.

Millett, J. D. "State Coordinating Boards and Statewide Governing Boards." In R. O. Berdahl (ed.), *Evaluating Statewide Boards.* New Directions for Institutional Research, no. 2. San Francisco: Jossey-Bass, 1975.

Mingle, J. R. "Effective Coordination of Higher Education: What Is It? Why Is It So Difficult to Achieve?" In L. F. Goodchild, C. D. Lovell, E. R. Hines, and J. I. Gill (eds.), *Public Policy and Higher Education.* Needham Heights, Mass.: Pearson Custom Publishing, 1997.

Mingle, J. R., and Epper, R. M. "State Coordination and Planning in an Age of Entrepreneurship." In L. F. Goodchild, C. D. Lovell, E. R. Hines, and J. I. Gill (eds.), *Public Policy and Higher Education.* Needham Heights, Mass.: Pearson Custom Publishing, 1997.

Nettles, M. T., Cole, J. K., and Sharp, S. "Assessment of Teaching and Learning in Higher Education and Public Accountability." National Center for Postsecondary Improvement, Stanford University, Stanford, Calif., 1997.

Perkins, J. A. "The New Conditions of Autonomy." In L. Wilson (ed.), *Emerging Patterns in Higher Education.* Washington, D.C.: American Council on Higher Education, 1965.

Richardson, R. C., Jr., Bracco, K. R., Callan, P. M., and Finney, J. E. *Designing State Higher Education Systems for a New Century.* Phoenix: Oryx, 1999.

Russell, A. B. *Issue Priorities and Trends in State Higher Education.* Denver: State Higher Education Executive Officers, 2000.

Southern Regional Education Board. "The 1995 Legislative Briefing." [http://www.sreb.org].

Southern Regional Education Board. "The 1997 Legislative Briefing." [http://www.sreb.org].

*State Postsecondary Education Structures Sourcebook*. Denver: Education Commission of the States, 1997.

"Steady Progress: Higher Education Governance in Colorado at the Dawn of the 21st Century." Report to the Colorado Department of Higher Education. Olympia, Wash.: Northwest Education Research Center, Nov. 2000.

Williams, D. T. "Efficiency and the Rise of State Coordinating Boards for Higher Education." Paper presented at the annual meeting of the Association for the Study of Higher Education, Washington D. C., Mar. 4–5, 1980. (ED 187 198)

*RUSSELL P. BUMBA, JR. is the senior manager for student services for the South Carolina Technical College System.*

3

*A good strategy for working with external media is
essential to the success of student affairs professionals.
Examples of practices that lead to effective engagement
with the various media are examined.*

# Student Affairs Professionals and the Media

*Ted Montgomery and Mary Beth Snyder*

"Nothing good ever happens after midnight" is a lesson learned early in the career of a student affairs professional. A ringing telephone in the middle of the night instantly signals the vice president, dean of students, or housing director that a serious problem—or worse, a crisis—is in the making back on campus. While the caller relates the facts, the vice president must begin formulating an appropriate response to the information, including an assessment of the potential for media interest.

The prominence of universities and colleges in their host communities virtually assures them of constant media attention. Over time, a symbiotic relationship develops between the campus and its correspondents: the university promotes positive media coverage of academic highlights, and, in turn, the media expects information access when the institution hits its inevitable low spots. And given their central role on campus, frequently students draw much of the media's attention. Their outstanding classroom accomplishments always are a source of public pride. However, reports of their misbehavior and unfortunate accidents also draw the campus into the media spotlight, especially when students' behavior stands in stark contrast to the professed values of the academy. Once rare, it is now expected that student affairs professionals will deal directly with broadcast and print media under both the best and the worst circumstances.

This chapter presents an overview of the essential elements of an external media relations' strategy for student affairs professionals. It discusses pitfalls and best practices, examines case situations, and draws workable conclusions. With forethought and practice, student personnel

NEW DIRECTIONS FOR STUDENT SERVICES, no. 100, Winter 2002  © Wiley Periodicals, Inc.

administrators can become instrumental in fostering a climate of trust with the media and, more important, in protecting the good name and reputation of their institutions.

## Community Engagement: Student Affairs and the Media

University engagement in the community via the media is essential. Every university is a big part of its community, and each one has many stories to tell. Beyond that there are other equally important reasons for universities to take purposeful steps to become engaged in media relations. First, the media will take an interest in campus life regardless of the institution's wishes; second, institutional involvement allows some control over the quality and accuracy of information; third, our involvement can help ensure an accurate understanding of the student and faculty experience in the community; fourth, it generates public goodwill; and finally, it allows taxpayers and state officials to learn and understand what is happening on campus.

As a major division of a university, the student affairs department has an obligation to participate in its campus media strategy. Every staff member should be prepared to deal with the media, for media calls rarely are funneled through one person in the department. Furthermore, student affairs professionals are in a unique position on their campuses. They are one of the only groups of university employees who interact regularly with student populations and the external media. This relationship can be mutually beneficial; student affairs professionals provide the media with interesting student stories and act as a direct conduit to the student body, while the media, in turn, can be persuaded to paint a positive picture of a university and its students. But the relationship is fraught with risks. Miscommunications, inattention to salient details, and adversarial relationships between certain students and administrators can hamstring the external relations goals of the university and cause a strained media relationship that might take years to repair. A common agenda must be created from the outset, and all student affairs staff must use that agenda as the blueprint from which to conduct their media relations efforts.

## The Rules of Media Engagement

A good campus media engagement program is distinguished by several factors, the most important of which is the creation of a long-term relationship based on mutual trust. This is achieved through careful adherence to some basic philosophies and practices.

**Stick to the Message.** Each campus has key messages, called *brag points,* that it wishes to disseminate with every media contact. These messages seek to give the university an image that clearly identifies it to students, parents, prospective students, alumni, donors, legislators, and the public at large. The student affairs staff should have a clear idea at all times of what the official university messages are and seek to emphasize them appropriately in every media contact. Repeating the "campus story" through media outlets serves as a constant reminder to business, industry, educational institutions, government, and community opinion leaders what one's campus and students truly stand for.

**Move the Students into the Community.** The student affairs division at each university is in a position to expose the media to select students by placing them in extracurricular activities in the community, especially in service-learning and media-related internships. Most universities with journalism schools place students in internships with newspapers, television news outlets, and radio stations. But even if a campus does not have a journalism school, encouraging students who are interested in public service and community activism to undertake an internship, especially with a news-gathering organization, is a good idea. Through such internships, students and their professors gain a clearer idea of what community engagement means and how campus life is interwoven with the fabric of the city. The media also will gain a clearer understanding of today's students and higher education in general.

**Know the Difference Between Rural and Urban Media Outlets.** The difference in media coverage of a rural versus an urban campus is considerable. In rural locales, news from the university often is a main source of stories for hometown newspapers. Many of these newspapers do not have sufficient staffing resources to cover their various beats as completely as they would like; as a consequence they may rely on student affairs professionals to feed them appropriate campus news and story ideas. Rural settings, especially predominantly farm communities, also typically have only one daily newspaper (and sometimes only weekly newspapers), making it easier for busy student affairs officers to keep all reporters in the current "information loop."

Urban campus settings, to the contrary, present far greater challenges for getting the university's message out through the media. Reporters in urban settings are less dependent on local university events for their daily newsgathering. They have city governments, businesses, schools, and professional sports teams about which to develop stories. When dealing with busy city reporters facing multiple deadlines it is essential for the student affairs official to have a keen sense for separating legitimate, interesting stories from ideas that will not be of interest to reporters. The quickest way, however, for a student affairs professional to lose the attention of a harried reporter is by constantly pitching uninteresting and nonnewsworthy stories.

**Team Up with Your Media Relations Officer.** Student affairs professionals stand on the front line of the relationship between students and the external media. They often are the first university representatives called by the media in times of campus crisis. At all times they should work with the university media relations department to craft appropriate responses to press inquiries.

The relationship between the student affairs professional and the media relations officer is an essential component of effective external communications. They must maintain regular, close contact and must apprise each other of developing situations likely to attract media inquiries. Working closely together they can issue statements and positions that reflect the official stance of the university on student-related issues, and ensure that the university becomes a well-prepared participant rather than a victim of the newsgathering process.

**Let Your Media Officer Run Interference.** The advantages to running all media inquiries initially through the media relations office are numerous. Often, that person is one of the few individuals on campus familiar with both the university community and the local media. He or she should always know about related articles and broadcast pieces that have been printed or aired, is likely to be acquainted personally with the reporter asking the questions, and will be able to avoid redundancies and the danger of conflicting comment from the university. Moreover, by knowing the reporter and news organization in question, the media relations officer will be better able to evaluate the likely angle and tone of the story.

**Get the Message Out.** Press releases are the most common form of getting the news out. The days of mailing press releases to the media are pretty much over. Faxing or e-mailing press releases to reporters is timelier and more targeted and will result in greater success. Even photographs that accompany press releases can be e-mailed to reporters without significant loss of clarity.

Radio interviews with students or student affairs professionals work well and often can be conducted by telephone. The added benefit of radio interviews is that if all goes well, the radio station host is likely to ask for a reappearance on future occasions.

Television interviews are trickier because for every ten minutes of footage shot, the station will normally use about forty-five seconds. Obviously such a deep edit can alter the context of what is said. When being interviewed by a television station it is best to keep one's comments brief and to try to make each sentence stand on its own in terms of clarity.

A relatively new form of communicating messages to external audiences is the campus Web site. Most Web sites include campus press releases. In addition, most good campus Web sites include a splash page for the department of student affairs. This is an effective way to get your messages to key audiences, including the media. It has the added advantage of being extremely timely as Web pages can be updated daily.

**Conduct Media Training.** To hone the media skills of key student affairs professionals and even students who may be interviewed frequently by the press, the media relations officer should hold media training sessions. This is a good way to gauge the interviewing skills of campus employees, who frequently are on camera, behind the microphone, or talking to reporters. A key part of this process is the so-called mock interview, which consists of interviewing the person being trained and videotaping the interview. This method allows you to critique the session and offer tips to the interviewee on how to improve his or her performance.

## Stepping Into the Spokesperson Role

A good relationship with the institution's chief media spokesperson virtually ensures that the vice president or dean of students and others will be called on to represent the university in the public spotlight. Moreover, since the media regard student affairs officers as their best conduit to the "student voice," they frequently will bypass the designated university official and go directly to the chief student-life administrator for comment.

**Put Yourself in the Loop.**  It is best for the chief student affairs officer to serve as a key member of a presidential leadership team that meets on a regular basis. The chief student affairs officer can represent the collective student viewpoint to other key university officials and foster discussion within the cabinet of issues vital to the student population and that affect the campus image. Conversely, student affairs staff must be informed fully about the institution's official position, if any, on issues that affect its well-being.

**Learn to Deal with the Print Media.**  The student affairs professional must be adept at and comfortable dealing with print media personnel. To accomplish this, it is recommended that the student affairs professional accompany the campus media relation's director on visits with the higher education beat writers of local newspapers. Regular contact with reporters is a strategic tactic essential to maintaining a good relationship with the press.

Keep in mind that when explaining university problems and policies to a reporter you will be talking to many people. It cannot be overemphasized that student affairs involvement in this process is a way to convey a clear message to student organizations, parents of students, other universities, the state legislature, and, of course, potential students.

*Meet the Press.*  At the initial meeting, the student affairs professional should inquire about what kind of stories each reporter is apt to be seeking from the university. Is there more interest in student success stories? Campus or dormitory life? Student government news? By asking the reporter this question, the student affairs professional helps establish a trusting relationship with the reporter for the future.

*Maintain Press Relationships.*  In subsequent conversations with the reporter the student affairs representative should be prepared to focus on what is happening on campus and to be brought up to date on what topics are possibly on the reporter's agenda. Sometimes the vice president or dean is able to offer insight on a story in progress or a point of view that the reporter has not considered.

The question of whether to give reporters a personal pager or home phone number has been debated at length. This invites the overzealous reporter to call you at home for information that is not vital or timely. However, by giving reporters these numbers, student affairs professionals are making themselves available to them at all times, a gesture of goodwill that is most appreciated.

*Encourage Advance Phone Calls from Reporters.* When reporters call the student affairs officer directly, they are usually looking for one of two things: to get an official university response to an issue, such as a campus crisis situation or an announced tuition increase, or to get the names of students to interview for a story. In either case, you have done a good job if reporters call before they come to campus or start seeking out students on their own. An advance call indicates that the reporter trusts and relies on the judgment of the campus official at critical times.

The concept of going off the record with a reporter has long been controversial. There are times when it is helpful to divulge certain information because it would be useful in enabling the reporter to get the story right, even though the person relating the information does not want the reporter to write about it. The best way to frame the information is to indicate to the reporter a willingness to go off the record in order to produce a more accurate story. It is important to note, however, that just saying, "This is off the record" before proceeding to relate inside information does not necessarily mean the reporter has agreed to treat what is said with discretion. There is no written code for how reporters treat off-the-record requests. The best approach is to get the reporter to agree to treat one's request to go off the record as just that—inside information that the reporter does not include in the article but that might be helpful in achieving accuracy. If the journalist does not agree to such a request and the discussion proceeds, then always expect what is said to wind up in print.

*Determine Whether to Seek Corrections or Let It Go.* Occasionally an article appears in the local paper with misquotes or quotes out of context. Depending on the importance of the issue, it is often a good idea to phone the reporter and explain your concern. An old adage states that you should never argue with those who buy ink by the barrel, and that is still true today. Make your case in a calm, reasoned manner, and never accuse the reporter of any sinister motives. If it is a matter of vital importance to the institution, it is well within your rights to ask for a correction or retraction or for another interview on the same topic. Most good reporters and editors will see the point if it is stated well, and will at least consider a correction. And even if they decline to print a correction, a call to them serves as notice that the campus is carefully evaluating its communications.

One note of caution: pick your spots carefully. Be careful not to acquire a reputation as someone who always calls a reporter to complain about quotes after an article has appeared; you will quickly lose credibility with the news organization in question. In many cases, the reporter frequently will avoid a particular source and cease calling for quotes. If this happens, the institution will have to make some serious repairs in its media relationships.

**Learn to Deal with the Electronic Media.** The electronic or broadcast media differ from the print media in that radio and television stations have much less time to tell their story. Consequently, they concentrate on provocative stories that titillate and often can be harmful to the institution. A recent case study at the authors' university serves as an example of the difficulties faced when working with broadcast media.

A situation occurred where a misreported story offered by a television news reporter turned into a media frenzy. The local TV news reporter got wind of a situation in which a woman student claimed that she had been raped in her dorm room. The resulting report intimated that there was an unknown rapist lurking in the bushes of our campus, when in fact the accuser knew her alleged assailant and actually was on a date with him on the night in question, during which both parties consumed large amounts of alcohol. Moreover, the campus police had already questioned the two students involved, along with many of their friends and acquaintances, about the events of the evening, and as a result of their inquiries, declined to even lodge a formal complaint against the alleged assailant.

The TV reporter took an interview she conducted with the complainant, who in declining to identify her alleged assailant gave the reporter the impression that he was an unknown person, and extrapolated her report to such a degree that it fanned the flames of campus panic. The result was that every media outlet in the area called to get details of this case, and each asked what we were doing to identify this "faceless rapist." In addition, because of the erroneous TV report, many parents—understandably—called to ask if their daughters were safe.

When the university explained the facts to the reporters, they declined to follow up on what they considered a case of "he said, she said" assault. Most reporters are reluctant to report a story of that sort until more reliable facts emerge. This unfortunate incident would never have happened if a newspaper reporter had handled it first or if the TV news reporter had gone through official university channels before interviewing the complainant. Any reliable reporter would talk to several sources before reporting an incendiary story like this; the TV reporter talked only to the complainant.

**Know the Differences Between Broadcast and Print Media.** The basic problem with television news outlets is that they have little time to get their stories, so they often cut corners. The blatantly misreported story described above forced the student affairs vice president to spend a day setting the record straight and caused undue concern among students and parents.

It is also more difficult to establish good relationships with television news reporters because the turnover of personnel on local news shows is so frequent, and because most TV reporters are not on a specific journalistic beat. The tactics suggested in the previous discussion about how to establish rapport with a newspaper reporter generally are not applicable in the case of TV news reporters.

The upside to electronic media coverage is that it is fairly easy to attract television crews to campus events that have a broad interest to television viewers, such as political rallies, specific celebrations, or a prominent guest speaker. Universities saw this in the aftermath of the terrorist tragedy of September 2001 when campus memorials and educational forums were attended by media wanting to show viewing audiences how young people were reacting to events.

The best way to get a television news crew to come to campus is to offer them opportunities tied to the general news events of the day. Be selective but persistent with broadcast media, knowing that they have a unique mission in journalism. When a national or campus crisis occurs, most television news organizations will send reporters to a campus without first alerting the student affairs office. But prior relationship-building efforts with TV personalities can serve the institution well when they arrive unannounced on campus with expectations of instant access.

## Balancing Openness with Student Privacy Rights

The Family Educational Rights and Privacy Act of 1974 (FERPA) established clear guidelines concerning confidential student educational records. Every student affairs professional and media relations expert must be completely familiar with these guidelines. Most reporters are uncertain as to what FERPA is and what can and cannot be disclosed to them regarding university students.

Student payment records, grades, conduct and incident reports, and personal information such as Social Security numbers, driver's license information, and family details are strictly off-limits to reporters. The sole exception to this rule occurs only if and when a student allows these records to be released to the media.

Often, reporters take an unexpected interest in a specific student matter. For example, at one time or another, every campus has encountered media curiosity surrounding the outcome of a student conduct case involving violent behavior. These are risky situations for the college because, on the one hand, the institution wants to reassure the public that the campus is safe while, on the other, it wants to protect the rights of all students involved by maintaining strict confidence about the details. Such cases can be used to educate the media about the differences between campus judicial systems and the criminal courts and about the protections afforded student information by federal and state laws. Donald Gehring (1999) provides an excellent description of college students' legal rights and offers advice on how to handle delicate situations in the public eye. Regardless of who serves as the institutional spokesperson in such incidents, that person must rely on the legal office for a current reading of the law pertaining to access to student information. Most intelligent reporters have good deductive abilities and are able to write a responsible story knowing just a simple fact such as whether a student remains enrolled.

## When Catastrophe Strikes

There is probably not a campus in the United States that has not had to deal with a crisis of some proportion. Often it is not the crisis itself, but rather how your campus community handles it that defines your preparedness for the situation. Fires, murder, assault, drunken driving incidents, riots, racially motivated violence, and dorm safety issues are all examples of crises that have occurred on American campuses through the years. Campus officials must handle each event swiftly, decisively, and delicately, and each will attract significant media attention.

**Always Be Prepared.**  The top two media priorities during these situations are (1) seeking to ensure that all information dispensed to the public and the media, on and off-campus, is accurate and (2) making certain that positive aspects of the university's response to the crisis are clearly and quickly relayed to the media.

One of the most essential aspects of handling a campus crisis is to be prepared before the crisis arises. Most universities have in place an established crisis communications team, with clearly defined goals for each team member relative to specific crisis situations. Without a well-rehearsed crisis communications team and plan already in place, chaos and confusion can rule on campus. Usually the media relations director is the point person for all media inquiries during a crisis. He or she acts as an information clearinghouse and liaison to other university officials.

**Know the Information Chain.**  The media relations officer will determine which university official will be the lead spokesperson during the crisis. Because so many crises involve students, the logical choice for an appropriate spokesperson often falls to the student affairs vice president or dean of students. That being the case, the student affairs professional becomes responsible for all intracampus communications during the time of crisis and for keeping students and staff apprised of the situation. He or she should be available to give regular updates to other university administration members, and should remain in regular contact with parents of students.

Work with the media relation's officer and other key administration officials to develop an official statement as soon as possible after the crisis has arisen. This statement should be updated and rereleased periodically as developments occur.

**Nip That Rumor in the Bud.**  The media will be hungry for any and all information it can get its hands on. At a time of crisis, rumors pose the greatest threat to the integrity of the official university statement. Naturally, students and staff talk about a crisis, often without having all the facts, and this is how rumors develop. The student affairs and media relations' officers must work in close collaboration to squelch rumors as they emerge in the campus dialogue. This is another reason why the official university statement should be frequently updated and issued to the media.

**Stick to the Verifiable Facts.** One thing that must always be foremost in the official spokesperson's mind during a crisis is to stay calm and never divulge information that has yet to be verified officially. Sometimes, in your zeal to squash rumors or shine a more positive light on a dire situation, you might be tempted to say things for publication that are not entirely true or as yet verified. This can undermine any crisis communications effort and have long-term negative ramifications throughout the campus community and beyond.

It is perfectly acceptable to tell a reporter that you do not know the answer to a particular question, but only with a promise to get the right answer and provide it right away. Most experienced reporters know that in crisis situations it usually takes a while for all the pertinent information to trickle in and to separate rumors from facts. A review of one serious campus crisis from the perspective of the former student affairs vice president in the midst of it, Dr. James Hurst, provides excellent instruction about what works well and not so well with respect to media relations during trying times.

## The University of Wyoming and the Matthew Shepard Tragedy

On a cold night in the fall of 1998 the University of Wyoming was rocked by the news that one of its students, twenty-one-year old Matthew Shepard, had been taken to the outskirts of the city of Laramie, tied to a fence, robbed, beaten, and left to die. While Matthew clung to life in the first hours after he was discovered, law enforcement officials quickly changed their initial crime identification from robbery to hate: Matthew was gay.

Early details about the hatefulness and brutality of the crime drew immediate media attention, and within hours of the news the University of Wyoming campus was ringed with every major news outlet from across the country. Even the president of the United States noted the ugliness of this hate crime in a national address.

In a personal e-mail exchange with Dr. James Hurst (November 21, 2001), one of the authors, Mary Beth Snyder, learned about valuable techniques to help the campus and the student affairs spokesperson weather the media storm during a crisis.

First, you must immediately designate someone to work with the press-media as a colleague to facilitate their getting the story they are seeking in the most accurate manner possible. Hurst concluded that the biggest mistake campuses make with the media is to treat them like the enemy, because they never seem to get the story right. At the University of Wyoming, they decided from the start to treat reporters as colleagues and to help them get accurate, up-to-the-minute information. The director of university relations must provide this kind of leadership from the moment a crisis hits. Hurst suggested that the campus establish "rumor control" centers across campus during a crisis and give heavy publicity to their existence. The creation of such centers requires collaboration by student affairs and media relations officers who must quickly train student and staff leaders to provide the correct information.

The media and the entire community appreciate periodic updates about the facts as they become known and about planned campus response to the crisis. Like most campuses, Wyoming had a crisis intervention team that held daily meetings in order to coordinate both the gathering and planned distribution of information to the media, which included sharing information that would provide a sense of comfort and security to the campus and community. Human-interest stories were abundant, and the campus felt that it was important to get these out quickly.

Hurst emphasized the importance of selecting articulate media spokespersons who, during a crisis, will define the values of the institution. In the Matthew Shepard case the president, vice president for student affairs, and the leaders of their lesbian and gay student associations served in that role. It was extremely helpful to have shown both the university president and campus student leaders at each other's side throughout the crisis, especially during press conferences.

Hurst stressed the additional strategy of distributing an information sheet to the community regarding how to interact with the press if approached. It contained information that included the right to not say anything along with encouragement to direct questions to the public relations, vice president's, or president's offices. Most individuals were more than happy to cooperate with that request. The piece also warned the campus about the few media persons who were there not to report the news but to create sensational stories that would attract attention and sell publications.

## Conclusion

The principles put forth in this chapter demonstrate that an intelligent and engaged media relations program, through the auspices of the campus student affairs department, is not only a smart idea but also practical and essential for effective community and media engagement. In today's news-hungry climate, university campuses are being looked at more frequently as a good source of stories for the media.

We have endeavored to demonstrate clearly what works best and what is to be avoided when dealing with the media. The changing face and ever-shifting priorities of the newsgathering operation requires all student affairs departments to develop a solid and workable plan for dealing with the media on a day-to-day basis.

## References

Bates, S. *If No News, Send Rumors: Anecdotes of American Journalism.* New York: St. Martin's Press, 1989.

*Dealing with the News Media.* Oakland University Communications and Marketing Department, Rochester, Mich.: Oakland University, 1998.

Fox, J. C., and Levin J. *How to Work With the Media.* Thousand Oaks, Calif.: Sage, 1993.

Gehring, D. "Do We Really Need All This Process?" Proceedings of the Twentieth Annual National Conference on Law and Higher Education, Stetson College of Law, 1999.

TED MONTGOMERY *is director of media relations at Oakland University in Michigan.*

MARY BETH SNYDER *is vice president for student affairs at Oakland University in Michigan.*

4

*Student affairs needs to be an active participant in campus decisions about corporate outsourcing partnerships to ensure that the effects of these relationships on student life are considered.*

# Do Corporate Outsourcing Partnerships Add Value to Student Life?

*James E. Moore*

Declining student enrollments, reductions in funding for higher education, and increased pressure to limit tuition have diminished revenue sources for colleges and universities. To remain competitive and to improve services, many institutions of higher education have increasingly turned to several popular business management approaches to perform internal tasks and functions (Wood, 2000; Kaganoff, 1998; Jefferies, 1996; Goodfriend, 2002). Student affairs staff have traditionally not been involved in the adoption of business strategies such as outsourcing. Since these strategies affect the campus learning environment, they affect students in some fashion. Student affairs staff need to adapt and become involved in these business decisions.

The trend to adapt to changing conditions began during the twentieth century, when college campuses stopped being entirely self-sufficient. Many institutions initially were located in rural settings far from city services and thus had to provide all of their own services (Bartem and Manning, 2001). As those campuses became increasingly surrounded by cities, they found that they had other options to performing necessary functions.

Advances in technology have also been an impetus. Trends in the business community have been another. As one of several business community management practices that became increasingly popular in higher education during the 1990s, the concept of outsourcing began to be applied to an increasing number of areas of the campus community. Prior to that time the primary outsourcing decisions concerned whether campus food services and the bookstore would be self-operated or contracted out. In addition, selected other functions were often contracted out—soda and snack vending

New Directions for Student Services, no. 100, Winter 2002   © Wiley Periodicals, Inc.

machines, game room equipment, and in some cases laundry machines—but primarily as a service to students. The idea of these functions becoming a revenue source, or of the providers of these functions becoming partners with a college or university, did not surface until recent years.

Economic conditions exert pressure on the world of business to look at its services, products, facilities, or functions with a dispassionate eye to decide whether they might be better performed by another organization (Bartem and Manning, 2001). The business community worked to reduce corporate bureaucracy in the 1980s. Massy and Meyerson (1997) reported that reengineered organizations focused on the core mission elements, which helped them to clarify what was essential about their organization. They suggested that this same approach would work in higher education. Functions that are not at the core of a college or university are good candidates for outsourcing. They note that companies have increasingly focused on their core mission, and have enjoyed success as they looked for alternative ways to accomplish peripheral functions.

During the 1990s, while under pressure from a variety of financial factors and influenced by governing board members from the corporate sector, many institutions of higher education began to explore some of these alternative methods to accomplish needed but more peripheral tasks. Business concepts such as downsizing, rightsizing, and economizing began to be applied to colleges and universities. Contract management evolved into concepts such as privatization and outsourcing (Goldstein, Kempner, Rush, and Bookman, 1993). While these terms still are used, in recent years additional practices have evolved, such as corporate service providers, auxiliary-vendor relationships, public-private partnerships, and corporate partnerships. While these terms are somewhat interchangeable, the partnership concept opens opportunities for increased involvement for student affairs staff.

## Deciding to Partner

What distinguishes a partnership with a corporate provider from the former contract management relationship? One way of looking at it is that contract management often tended to be more of a one-way relationship, with the university purchasing a particular service. Corporate partnerships tend to be two-way relationships. Each partner needs to contribute its expertise to the particular function, each also needs to give up some control, and then each needs to trust the other partner to fulfill their end of the deal. Partnerships tend to be value-added, with each partner contributing to the relationship. Although it is obvious that the institution would be looking for the value that prospective partners would add to the university service operation, it has also been suggested that the university should ask the corporate partner what value the university adds to its corporate operation (Scherrens, 1999). From this perspective, each partner maintains a learning-centered, results-oriented perspective.

Several authors have suggested strategies to help a campus determine if an outsourced, corporate partnership is an appropriate choice for that institution (e.g., Goldstein, Kempner, Rush, and Bookman, 1993; Jefferies, 1996; Massy and Meyerson, 1997; Wertz, 1997; Peterson's Guides, 1995; Kaganoff, 1998; Riley, 2000; Wood, 2000; Moneta and Dillon, 2001; and Scherrens, 1999). The systems approach described by Scherrens may prove most useful to the student affairs officer.

According to Scherrens, in order to know which service areas have the best potential to develop a partnership relationship, an institution needs to know the range of possible services on campus; be able to articulate a rationale for doing each of them; understand the relationship of each service to the core university mission of teaching and learning; be able to evaluate the current performance of the services; learn about and get to know the fields of the different services for examples of best practice; and then decide on a course of action. This decision could involve restructuring the service, discontinuing it, outsourcing it, or continuing with the current operation (Scherrens, 1999). What is central to this approach, and to the advice of the other authors cited above, is that an institution should focus on its mission, be clear about its central processes, and be willing to adapt its noncore functions to changing economic and environmental factors. This includes being open to the concept of outsourcing.

Most of the impetus for identifying alternative sources for these services and functions has come from the campus business officer. Therefore, most of the literature on these topics is found at organizations such as the National Association of College and University Business Officers and the National Association of Campus Auxiliary Services (NACAS). Very little information on the issues of outsourcing or partnerships was evident in the literature of student affairs until the publication of a monograph on external partnerships by Dietz and Enchelmayer (2001). While student affairs staff can learn valuable lessons from campus business office colleagues, it is important for the student affairs leadership to understand how decisions to enter into a corporate partnership might affect student life on the campus and then to ensure that the student perspective is factored into the partnership decision-making process.

Given the growth in the number and variety of outsourced corporate partnerships within the past decade, information on the topics of outsourcing, privatization, and partnerships has started to increase. In response to the interest in this topic, the National Association of College Auxiliary Services created an electronic web site on this subject. The Center for the Study of Outsourcing and Privatization in Higher Education was formed in 2001. This site can be reached through the NACAS home page, or directly at http://www.csophe.net. If it lives up to its promise, the site should continue to have up-to-date information about many issues that relate to the topics of outsourcing and partnership relationship.

## Reasons to Partner

According to a 2001 survey of business officers, 6 percent of colleges and universities do not outsource any functions, while 50 percent outsource only one to three services. The top five services that were contracted were food service (75 percent), vending (63 percent), bookstore (46 percent), custodial service of academic buildings (26 percent), and laundry (21 percent). The top reasons colleges and universities chose to outsource were better equipment, time-savings, cost containment, operations improvement, and professional management (Argon, 2001).

Although these reasons may include multiple meanings to the survey respondents, noticeably absent from this listing are any student life factors. Such factors might include improved service to students, impact on the learning environment, meeting student needs better, and improving student satisfaction. All of these factors can be campus retention issues.

Some institutions have chosen to outsource campus functions because the corporate partner has creativity and specialized knowledge that is beneficial to the institution. In addition, because corporate partners often operate at multiple institutions, they have access to strong managers who are willing to move to a new campus for career advancement. The institution thus benefits from the human resources of the corporate partner. The contracted management team also has access to the latest human resources, management, and fiscal developments in the field (Bartem and Manning, 2001).

Broad (1998) notes five reasons to develop partnerships in the information technology field:

- *Timeliness:* The institution gains the resources and expertise to adapt quickly to changes in technology.
- *Currency:* The institution is able to bring its technological infrastructure up to date.
- *Risk sharing:* Given the rate of change in the field of technology, the costs of retooling infrastructure are shared. This element of risk serves as a major incentive for the partners to work together.
- *Matching competencies:* Each partner can benefit from the organizational and operational strengths of the other.
- *Revenue opportunities:* By relying on each other's strengths, both partners may realize financial gain.

These five reasons also apply to other partnership endeavors. In the field of technology, other possibilities for partnerships are evolving. For example, some institutions are considering whether to become institution partners with a "campus portal" provider. This decision may depend on how closely the institution decides those virtual access services relate to its core mission.

## Reasons Not to Partner

Some people in higher education have concerns about outsourcing and partnership relationships. One of the factors noted by Wood (2000), Ender and Mooney (1994), and others relates to a variety of human resources issues. These concerns include university employees losing their jobs or, if employees are retained by the corporate partner, losing their benefits or being paid a lower salary. These retained employees, now working for the new corporate partner, may begin to feel like second-class citizens on campus. Some have suggested that corporate partner staff have less loyalty to the institution than university employees. Another human resources issue could be the morale of other university workers, who might wonder if their position will be the next function to be outsourced.

Another reason cited is that businesses run as profit centers (Bartem and Manning, 2001). Businesses look at costs, including human resources, differently from the way many colleges and universities do. If the culture and norms of the potential partner are not well understood, the values of the corporate and educational partners may be at odds. For this reason, Scherrens (1999) advises that potential partners be researched thoroughly.

To students, the human dynamics of some partner decisions may be significant. Students may visit daily with a food service checker who knows the name of every student entering the cafeteria, a housekeeper who jokes with students while working, or a grounds crew member who demonstrates pride in the appearance of the campus physical environment. Each of these individuals may have a significant and positive effect on the lives of students. If the custodial function in academic buildings is contracted, and it is decided to perform the work in the early evening hours, is valuable student study space disrupted?

Some institutions have considered outsourcing the campus police force. The rationale in favor of outsourcing may relate to efficiency, a lack of available staffing, better trained off-campus officers, lower equipment expenditures, or more professional management. Another reason might be to facilitate better coordination with other local law enforcement agencies.

Other institutions have judged that a campus police-public safety department is a very different entity from a community police force. Campus police officers usually develop special relationships with students, often knowing them on a first-name basis. Campus officers understand the mission of the institution and support it in the performance of their jobs. Since student affairs staff members are the individuals who usually are called in the middle of the night to respond to student misbehavior, it helps to personally know and help train the officers who make the judgments about whether to refer a student to the student discipline system, have the student arrested, or take the student home.

Another factor that should be considered in some outsourcing decisions is the potential for student activism in protest of the partner. Might students react negatively to a food service provider that also supplies food to a local prison, or to the labor practices of a food provider for the campus food service? A number of campuses have dealt with student criticism of school-affiliated clothing being made in "sweatshop" conditions in Third World countries.

Although the issues cited above should not make or break a potential partnership, they should be considered in the decision-making process. The leadership of student affairs should know about these and other aspects of student life as they influence the satisfaction and retention of students. To incorporate this type of information into the partnership decision-making process, a good collaborative relationship needs to exist between business affairs and student affairs.

## Student Affairs Partnerships

In student affairs, one area that has seen a dramatic change in the past decade has been campus housing. Historically most colleges and universities have owned and operated their own housing facilities (while using a private firm to design and construct the buildings). A new practice of creating fully privatized, ground-lease partnership arrangements began to increase during the 1990s. This practice involved the development, ownership, and management of the facility being outsourced to a private developer, with the net revenues shared between the developer and the university. The late 1990s gave rise to the practice of university-affiliated nonprofit corporations—which used ground-lease arrangements, where the nonprofit corporation outsourced the development and management of the facility to a third party. At some institutions, the partnership arrangement was based on establishing a nonprofit corporation not affiliated with the institution, with the corporation developing and managing the housing facility (Anderson, 2001).

Although universities still partnered with private developers, by 2001 the relationships became more complex. The new partnerships began to be structured for the mutual benefit of the developer and the university. One example of this change is evident in how housing projects were funded. In the latter half of the 1990s about half of the housing projects were built with tax-exempt financing. By 2001 about 80 percent of campus housing projects were again financed through tax-exempt bonds (Baltic, 2001). This shift back to housing projects being funded increasingly by colleges and universities was influenced by external scrutiny of the off-balance-sheet financing arrangements through nonprofit corporations. The IRS questioned whether some of the nonprofit corporations were truly independent of the university. In addition, bond-rating agencies increasingly factored in how much a particular project would affect the institution's debt capacity, regardless of its nonprofit arrangement (Baltic, 2001).

Some universities have terminated their outsourced student housing relationships because they did not deliver on the original expected benefits of partnership. At one institution, the arrangement to outsource maintenance and housekeeping of the campus residence halls did not work because of a significant backlog of deferred maintenance. The university understood that the partnership would not work if the corporate partner lost money, so the contract was renegotiated (Van Der Werf, 2000).

Another student life outsourcing function is addressed in a report on career services in the United Kingdom. It notes that budget pressures and recent changes in the structures of work and careers have resulted in the need to reconsider the role of career services in higher education (Watts, 1997). Seven strategic directions for career services are identified. Four—the integrated guidance model, the integrated placement model, the curriculum model, and the learning organization model—are considered to be strongly embedded within the university. Three—the extended support model, the lifelong guidance model, and the alumni model—are based on delivering career services after graduation. Depending on the defined mission of the institution, the latter three models might be viable candidates for an outsourced partner relationship.

Finally, the function of counseling services is addressed in one student affairs journal. Webb, Widseth, and John (1997) note that colleges and universities must consider proposals to outsource counseling and psychological services in the context of their individual mission. They must also consider what society, parents, and students regard as a contract with students and their families. The authors note that campus mental health professionals have many roles to play beyond just mental health counseling and psychotherapy. They participate on committees, conduct educational outreach programs, and consult with faculty and staff about students. These tasks require an understanding of and allegiance to the values and mission of the institution. They note that outsourcing proposals promise to save money, but they ask "at what cost?" From their perspective, counseling services are a necessary core service of a college or university and not good candidates for outsourcing to an off-campus partner.

## Reasons for Student Affairs Involvement in Partnership Decisions

The development of a sense of campus community has been an important function for student affairs. This is one reason for staff in the field to be involved as an on-campus partner in creating relationships with off-campus service providers. Most of these partnerships affect students. Student affairs staff members are, or should be, experts on the needs of students, as well as experts on creating and sustaining a sense of community on the campus.

Banning (1999) provides a connection between those on campus who are primarily concerned with financial matters and those who are concerned with attracting, retaining, and graduating students. He notes that campus facilities can communicate a sense of space. This "place attachment" may be looked at as a "combination of characteristics that make a place special or unique. The characteristics include physical setting affect, cognition (memories, expectations, previous experience, meanings symbols) and activities" (p. 16). Banning also cites others (Reeve and Kassabaum, 1997, p. 219) who note that a "sense of place refers to our human, emotional response to the qualities of physical spaces." The point is that our facilities and services communicate varying degrees of sense of place. Students react to those messages by either wanting to be in that space or not wanting to be there. Banning notes that the degree to which auxiliary facilities can contribute to the campus' sense of space, the more students will be attracted to the campus and will feel a sense of belonging and desire to participate. Banning notes that the physical design of a campus plays a critical role in fostering, or not fostering, a sense of community.

By extension, the design and delivery of partnership services can convey a sense of belonging and attachment. Because these are crucial concerns for student satisfaction and retention, they provide a strong justification for student affairs staff to be intimately involved in the identification, development, and oversight of those partnership arrangements that affect student life.

Student affairs staff also should be involved in the partnership enterprise because the reality of declining resources affects all areas of the institution. In addition, accountability questions, benchmarking comparisons, and "quality improvement" challenges are already happening—sometimes imposed by external mandate and sometimes at the directive of institutional leadership. Student affairs leaders should be active players in this dialogue and not let these external factors limit their ability to create and sustain a vibrant campus learning community for students.

## Lessons Learned

A partnership is based on a relationship. To forge and sustain a good partnership, consider what it takes to maintain a good relationship. Common values, shared interests and similar goals, time spent together, effective communications, and a mutually beneficial relationship are essential elements in developing a partnership. How might these relationship elements be reflected in a corporate partnership? Additional advice on how to create and maintain a partnership is noted in the section that follows, based in part on suggestions from Scherrens (1999).

Values are reflected in the culture of organizations. Before deciding to outsource, the culture and values of the division and university must be understood. This self-analysis is essential to ensure that the culture and values of the future partner mesh with those of the university.

In addressing these questions, it is important that more than one area on campus be included in this analysis. All affected parties should be involved in this review. Each area offers a valuable perspective in defining the culture of the campus and its reasons for seeking a business partnership. If differences of opinion emerge within the institution, it would be better to address and resolve them before going out for a bid. This approach avoids the uncomfortable situation of putting an external partner in the middle of internal disagreements.

After assessing its culture, an institution should define the reasons for wanting to outsource and state these expectations clearly. Does the university desire a greater level of service than is currently provided? Does it seek a higher financial return? Does it lack sufficient expertise in this area? What are the expected outcomes? Prospective business partners will need to know what the institution wants in order to determine if and how to submit a proposal. Successful business organizations will engage in a similar review of the culture of their business and the reasons for partnering with the institution.

When the university evaluates proposals, it is crucial that the key decision makers learn as much as possible about the business culture of the bidder. How do they treat their own people? How do they operate on other campuses? What is their motivation for bidding, and what do they hope to get out of this relationship? Would this just be one more account, or does the prospective partner treat the institution as special and important? After learning about the culture of each organization, assess how each would mesh with the culture of the institution. Ensure that the culture of the business serves the culture of the university (Bartem and Manning, 2001; Scherrens, 1999).

A key factor in knowing how the culture of the business will be reflected on campus is in the personnel who will be working on the campus. It is highly beneficial that the finalists being considered be expected to indicate who will be the individuals involved in managing the campus partnership. These individuals should be interviewed as if they were an institutional hire. As the university gets to know them, it will acquire additional information about how well the culture and interests of the business partner will be reflected in the day-to-day operation of its relationship with the campus.

Once a decision is made to engage a partner, the institution needs to decide how it wants to sustain communications. These expectations need to be included in the contract. How often will key people meet? What kinds of reports are expected and when are they expected? Who speaks for each partner? Although it is important to be clear about how to handle formal communications, it is also essential to develop a means of frequent informal communications. This will help to sustain and nourish the relationship, as well as provide early notice of potential problems that need to be addressed.

If there is a long-term agreement, it is important, on an annual basis at a minimum, to set and review the goals and expectations of the partnership. Is the partnership proceeding as it was projected? Have business conditions changed, necessitating a modification in the agreement? Have personnel changed and do these new human dynamics require other adjustments?

In some partnership arrangements a corporate partner may have an inclination to report only good news. If an institution suspects that it is not hearing the full story, it would be advisable to engage an independent expert to evaluate the pertinent physical facilities, financial picture, programs offered, or services provided. The institution should also conduct periodic satisfaction surveys of campus stakeholders of partnership relationships.

As with successful personal relationships, look for ways to meet and exceed the expectations of the partner. Perhaps the institution could offer the partner tickets to athletic events. Perhaps a book on motivation will be meaningful to the manager of the account. Improving partner satisfaction and having the partner know that the university is concerned about its interests will increase the odds that it will act in a like manner toward the institution. Look for ways to exceed minimum expectations. Look for things that can be learned from the corporate partner. Have fun and enjoy the relationship.

Based on extensive experience in creating, maintaining, and evaluating service provider relationships, Scherrens (1999) addressed the issue of "lessons learned" from a similar perspective. He noted that campuses should maintain communication on a routine and regular basis, foster joint ownership and responsibility for both the process and the product, and understand and respect the fact that the organizational objectives of the partners are not the same.

Scherrens also noted that the biggest challenge for most institutions is to share rather than control their decision-making responsibility, while not losing sight of ultimate institutional accountability, that partners with a passion for perfection understand the need for sharing a common knowledge base, and that information not shared between partners is useless data. It is important for partners to strive for value-added partnerships, with each partner contributing something of value to the relationship, and to strive for continuous improvement.

An informal survey by the author of corporate partners and colleagues in higher education provided feedback that was remarkably consistent. From both perspectives the advice provided was that it is crucial to maintain good lines of communication, that a partnership will work if partners develop a trusting relationship, and that a key to a successful partnership is the quality of the managers who are directly responsible for the daily operation of the partnership.

It was also noted that it makes more sense to maintain a relationship with candid feedback than to constantly go out for bids, and to recognize that the university and the business partner have different, yet interdependent, interests; and that if institutional feedback does not produce the desired results, and/or the partner is not willing to change managers or practices, the university should change partners.

## Conclusion

Partnerships with off-campus service providers can bring valuable expertise to the delivery of particular services on campus. The synergy of different perspectives can improve the quality of the final product. This same approach applies on campus. Student affairs leaders should take the initiative to collaborate or partner with business office representatives, students, faculty, and other staff in the review of services and programs and the development of partnership planning teams. On-campus partnerships can improve service as well as develop positive working relationships.

When an institution considers forming a corporate outsourcing partnership it is crucial that the impact of that relationship on student life be considered. Student affairs staff members need to assume that a leadership role on campus is addressing how the proposed partnership will affect students. Partnership decisions that only consider financial aspects have the potential to create a negative impact on student life. Student affairs staff should ensure that proposed outsourcing partnerships affect student life in a positive manner.

## References

Anderson, L. "Campus Housing Retrospective: The Evolution of Public/Private Partnerships for Student Housing." *College Services,* April 2001, 20–23.

Argon, J., "Keeping It Close to Home." *American School and University,* 2001, 74(1), 24–28.

Baltic, S., "Designer Dorms." *University Business,* 2001, 4(7), 34–41, 70–71.

Banning, J. H. "Campus Facility Design: Lessons from the 20th Century and Implications for the 21st." *College Services Administration,* 1999, 22(4), 16–19.

Bartem, R., and Manning, S. "Outsourcing in Higher Education: A Business Officer and Business Partner Discuss a Controversial Management Strategy." *Change,* 2001, 33(1), 42–47.

Broad, M. C. "Strategic Partnerships: What Universities and Corporations Can Do Together." In C. L. Bernard, S. L. Johnson, J. J. Kidwell, and PricewaterhouseCooper (eds.), *Reinventing the University: Managing and Financing Institutions of Higher Education.* New York: Wiley, 1998.

Dietz, L. H., and Enchelmayer, E. J. (eds.). *Developing External Partnerships for Cost-Effective, Enhanced Service.* New Directions for Student Services, no. 96. San Francisco: Jossey-Bass, 2001.

Ender, K. L., and Mooney, K. A. "From Outsourcing to Alliances: Strategic Strategies for Sharing Leadership and Exploiting Resources at Metropolitan Universities." *Metropolitan Universities: An International Forum,* 1994, 5(3), 51–60.

Goldstein, P. J., Kempner, D. E., Rush, S. C., and Bookman, M. *Contract Management or Self-Operation: A Decision-Making Guide for Higher Education.* Washington, D.C.: Council of Higher Education Management Associations, 1993. (ED 375 704)

Goodfriend, H. J. "What Has Happened to Outsourcing in Higher Education? A Close Look at the Current State of Outsourcing and Privatization in Higher Education." *College Services,* 2002, 18–23.

Jefferies, C. L. "The Privatization Debate: Examining the Decision to Outsource a Service." *Business Officer,* 1996, *29*(7), 26–30.

Kaganoff, T. "Collaboration, Technology and Outsourcing Initiatives in Higher Education: A Literature Review." Foundation for Independent Higher Education, 1998. (ED 420 289)

Massy, W. F., and Meyerson, J. W. (eds.). *New Models for Higher Education.* Princeton, N.J.: Peterson, 1997.

Moneta, L., and Dillon, D. L. "Strategies for Effective Outsourcing." In L. H. Dietz and E. J. Enchelmayer (eds.), *Developing External Partnerships for Cost-Effective, Enhanced Service.* New Directions for Student Services, no. 96. San Francisco: Jossey-Bass, 2001.

National Association of College Auxiliary Services. The Center for the Study of Outsourcing and Privatization in Higher Education Web site, [http://www. csophe.net].

Peterson's Guides. *Peterson's Contract Services for Higher Education.* The Directory of Outsource Service Vendors for College and Universities. Princeton, N.J.: Peterson, 1995. (ED 405 787)

Reeve, I. R., and Kassabaum, D. G. "A Sense of Place Master Plan: Linking Mission and Place." APPA Proceedings, 1997, 219–228.

Riley, J. F. "Chapter 17, Procurement." In C. Grills (ed.), *College and University Business Administration* (6th ed.). Washington, D.C.: National Association of College and University Business Officers, 2000.

Scherrens, M. W. *Maximizing Service Provider Relationships: Best Practices Through Blended Management.* Washington, D.C.: National Association of College and University Business Officers, 1999.

Van Der Werf, M. "How the University of Pennsylvania Learned That Outsourcing Is No Panacea." *Chronicle of Higher Education,* Apr. 7, 2000, *46*(31), A38–39.

Watts, A. G. "Strategic Directions for Career Services in Higher Education." Cambridge, Eng.: Association of Graduate Careers Advisory Services; National Institute for Careers, Education and Counselling, 1997.

Webb, R. E., Widseth, J. C., and John, K. B. "Outsourcing and the Role of Psychological Services on College Campuses." *NASPA Journal,* 1997, *34*(3), 186–198.

Wertz, R. D. "Outsourcing and Privatization of Campus Services: An Overview and Guide for College and University Administrators." Charlottesville, Va.: National Association of College Auxiliary Services, 1997.

Wood, P. A. "Outsourcing in Higher Education," *ERIC Digest,* 2000. (ED 446 726)

*JAMES E. MOORE is assistant vice president for student services at Creighton University in Omaha, Nebraska.*

5

*Alumni organizations have special opportunities to
influence the experience of prospective and current college
students. This chapter explores programs that enhance
connections between students and alumni.*

# The Role of the Alumni Association in Student Life

*Tara S. Singer and Aaron W. Hughey*

Several years ago, one of the authors of this chapter was preparing to interview for the position of alumni director. She searched the library for information that might be helpful in an interview situation. Coming from a student affairs background, she naturally assumed that the format and substance of the search process would be similar. For example, because student affairs professionals had meticulously constructed and routinely used various theories of student development in their management and programming initiatives, it was naively believed that alumni relations professionals might follow a similar model. Like their institutional counterparts, surely professionals in the alumni relations field had cultivated and finely tuned multiple theories of alumni development.

She soon realized that this was not the case. *Development,* it appeared, had an entirely different connotation when used within the context of alumni affairs. In alumni affairs, a field inherently intertwined with institutional advancement, when colleagues spoke of development, they were talking about raising money. They were *not* talking about the moral, intellectual, or psychosocial constructs that she had spent fifteen years learning, researching, discussing, and implementing in daily professional tasks. Within the scope of alumni affairs, *alumni* are merely students who have graduated. True, they are often older, more robust, grayer, and sometimes balder, but they are also generally wiser and financially better off than they were as undergraduates. In any event, they still have an integral and inseparable connection to the institution from which they received a degree.

At the same time, the author quickly found that the same knowledge and skills that were so useful in designing and facilitating activities in the student affairs arena translated very nicely into planning special events for alumni. The time spent nurturing student leaders and coordinating the efforts of campus volunteers turned out to be invaluable in working with alumni in the ongoing process of building communities and connections. Moreover, the courses that she had taken in adult education proved to be instrumental in understanding and meeting the unique needs of alumni who increasingly are recognizing the value of learning as a lifelong pursuit.

Within most colleges and universities, alumni affairs professionals engage in a number of different strategies aimed at helping them to become productive partners with other campus groups in their collective goal to enhance and enrich student life. In this chapter, we explore some of the more relevant and influential theories that attempt to address the relationship between the student and alumni experience. We also describe a variety of different programs that successfully bring students and alumni together for their mutual benefit. Finally, we discuss the institutional benefits associated with colleges and universities that sponsor and support these kinds of collaborative programs.

## Background

In recent years, colleges and universities have become much more cognizant of the tremendous advantages associated with orienting and integrating academic affairs, student affairs, and alumni services toward common goals and objectives. Indeed, numerous opportunities exist for student affairs professionals to form partnerships with their colleagues in alumni affairs. Both areas are concerned with enhancing the image of the institution and the experience of those who have contact with it. They strive to accomplish these objectives by working with essentially the same population—but at different points in their association with the campus. Where this kind of synergistic cooperation has been fostered and maintained, the benefits for both student and alumni affairs have been considerable.

Today's student and alumni affairs professionals are actively engaged in a number of mutually beneficial institutional activities on behalf of students. These collaborative efforts include programs designed to improve the overall quality of student life, strategies designed to orient and welcome new students to the campus, and initiatives designed to attract students to, and subsequently retain them within, the institution (Garland and Grace, 1994). Success in these fundamental endeavors is critical to institutions that aspire to maintain strong enrollments of qualified students, guarantee high levels of academic quality and achievement, and ensure that graduates are successful in obtaining appropriate employment once they receive their diplomas. Alumni who have a strong sense of the mission of the institution from which they graduated, and are visibly supportive of that mission in a variety of tangible ways, are essential to achieving all of these goals.

Evolving economic and cultural realities require academic profession-als who are competent in a variety of complementary and interrelated skills, including counseling and administration, organizational development, qual-ity management, planning, evaluation and research, and familiarity with current issues in higher education (Garland and Grace, 1994). It is becom-ing increasingly evident that student and alumni affairs professionals must work creatively and in concert with each other if the institution's total well-being is to be integrated effectively with that of its students. One of the prin-cipal advantages precipitated by greater collaboration between alumni and student affairs is the opportunity that such collaboration affords to share resources that are becoming increasingly scarce at many colleges and uni-versities. In essence, the efficient sharing of key assets (including operating costs and personnel) is becoming more of a necessity than a luxury within institutions that are working to provide programs and services that are effec-tive both now and in the future. In higher education, cooperation really is an indispensable prerequisite to continual improvement.

Partnerships between student and alumni affairs can provide students with significant opportunities for growth and development. Kellogg (1996) investigated the extent to which true collaboration exists between student and alumni affairs. Most student and alumni affairs professionals report that their experiences are primarily positive when programs are planned coop-eratively. Professionals from both areas indicate that when the target pop-ulation for a program includes both students and alumni, these gatherings generally have very rewarding results. Several avenues exist for student and alumni affairs professionals to work collaboratively. What follows is a dis-cussion of some strategies that have been used to strengthen the connection between students, alumni, and their institutions. The inherent value of sev-eral of these programs has been questioned seriously in the past, but the current economic and social climate is causing a discernible shift in the atti-tudes of many regarding their importance to the institution.

## Involving Alumni in Admissions

Many colleges and universities have adopted programs that involve alumni directly in the recruitment of prospective students in conjunction with admissions offices. Hanson (2000) found that several factors accurately pre-dict which alumni are most likely to promote their institutions to others. These factors include organizational prestige, social identification, years since graduation, and respect for alumni leaders. Most colleges and univer-sities actively use their institutional rituals and traditions to recruit prospec-tive students. These institutional beliefs often are accepted and actively supported by parents, faculty, and especially alumni. In any event, the key to any recruitment strategy that involves alumni seems to be the identifica-tion of factors that tend to influence the formation of a close relationship between the institution, its current students, and its alumni (Kellogg, 1996).

In reality, alumni can, and probably should, be involved extensively in all phases of student recruitment, admissions, and the orientation process. Institutions that offer their alumni opportunities for involvement benefit graduates by providing not only meaningful volunteer service experiences but current information on academic program offerings, student life events, and campus activities. And as they work to maintain and even enhance enrollments at their alma mater, these kinds of experiences often serve to enrich the lives of alumni in myriad ways. Regardless of how involved the alumni association is with various recruitment and admissions activities, Dolbert (2000) strongly recommends that the primary coordination of these efforts remain within the admissions unit. Since this is their primary focus, admissions professionals are obviously in the best position to oversee and monitor the institution's total recruitment program.

**Undergraduate Recruitment.**  Alumni admissions programs vary in scope from institution to institution. At many schools, alumni admissions volunteers work individually to host student recruitment activities in their homes and represent their schools at "college night" programs. Alumni, particularly those who had a very positive experience as undergraduates at the college or university, may be asked to speak or write to prospective students in their communities about their undergraduate experiences and encourage prospective students to consider attending the institution after completing high school. Lynchburg College, for example, has developed an excellent alumni recruitment program that attempts to engage all of its past graduates. Each year, its admissions office, working closely with alumni relations, sends view books, applications, and referral cards to all living alumni. The alumni are encouraged to share these materials with prospective students whom they believe would be academically qualified and interested in Lynchburg College. Through this mailing and various follow-up measures, graduates are asked to help the school identify the next generation of students. In addition to the obvious benefit to Lynchburg College, alumni who participate in the program tend to retain a close connection to the institution, which benefits everyone.

In contrast to the fairly comprehensive approach taken by Lynchburg College, many colleges and universities involve only a highly select group of alumni in the recruitment of prospective students. Representative of the schools that take such an approach is Pennsylvania State University. At Penn State, alumni admissions volunteers register to assist in the identification of high-achieving students who might have an interest in the school. They also serve as a resource to local high school guidance counselors by providing various recruitment and admissions materials that subsequently are distributed to potential Penn State students. The alumni admissions volunteers also call to congratulate students who have been offered admission to the institution, as well as assist with determining who should receive one of the university's merit-based scholarships. The program is popular among the institution's graduates, who regard it as an honor. At the present time, well over one thousand Penn State alumni are actively working as admissions volunteers.

Dolbert (2000) indicates that a well-developed training program for alumni volunteers is essential, particularly if an institution is engaging these alumni in the recruitment and selection of high-achieving students. While many institutions provide their alumni admissions volunteers with general recruitment materials, colleges and universities that want to maximize the impact of these individuals should consider providing them with more detailed and descriptive information on financial aid, merit-based scholarships, academic programs, and, last but certainly not least, student housing. Moreover, many schools conduct on-campus workshops for their alumni volunteers. These workshops allow the alumni to share information and insights as well as to ask questions about any recent changes in admissions requirements and other campus policies and procedures. Other topics frequently incorporated into the workshops include a discussion of the appropriate tactics for hosting a successful recruitment program or send-off party, and how the desired student population profile may be evolving with respect to both major and minor changes in the institutional mission. As an added benefit to the alumni volunteers, the workshops provide graduates with an occasion to reacquaint themselves with the campus, visit with former professors and staff, and engage in some excellent career networking.

**Admissions Selection.**  At highly selective institutions, alumni volunteers often help the admissions office by participating in interviews with students who have applied to the school. These interviews provide admission committees with important information about prospective students that might not have been conveyed through their written applications and admissions essays. Although very useful information can be gleaned from applications, essays, and test scores, there is no real substitute for personal interaction as an evaluative technique. A good example is Washington University in St. Louis, which involves both alumni as well as parents of current students in interviewing prospective candidates. These interviews help determine if a student is a good match with the institution, and also can serve to help strengthen a student's interest in the university. It is no secret that students often apply to a number of different institutions when trying to decide where to continue their education. If a student is truly undecided about where to attend school, a personal interview, or even a telephone call, from an alumni volunteer might be the just the thing that causes them to commit. The effect can be even more profound if the alumni volunteer making the contact majored in the prospective student's anticipated subject area or career field. Available technology allows this to be facilitated with minimal effort at most institutions.

**Welcome and Orientation Programs.**  After a student has been accepted and has decided to attend a particular institution, alumni organizations can play a key role in the process of orienting the new recruit to college. Many institutions routinely collect data regarding the perceptions of their graduating seniors and alumni concerning the extent to which academic, personal, social, and vocational goals were met while in college. The perspectives of alumni can be invaluable to new students as they learn to negotiate the campus environment and make decisions that have the potential to make an impact on their collegiate as well as postcollegiate careers. These types of alumni-student interactions, when facilitated in conjunction with orientation activities, provide students with the opportunity to learn from alumni while developing greater loyalty to the institution.

Many alumni organizations coordinate send-off or welcome parties for incoming students. These events usually are held during the summer months and are hosted either by individual alumni admissions volunteers or by regional alumni clubs. These events are good settings for providing students and their parents with final information on housing assignments, financial aid packages, and course schedules. They provide a venue for the incoming students to identify the individuals in their communities who are already graduates of their new school. They also may be used to help introduce new students to other currently enrolled students as well as parents to other parents and alumni.

Among the more innovative programs developed by student affairs and alumni organizations are those designed to communicate the campus culture to new students. At the University of Texas, for example, each year the Texas Exes sponsor a three-day retreat known as Camp Texas, which is designed to orient incoming freshmen to the "Longhorn" way of life. As is noted on the Camp Texas web site, the program is not intended to replace, or be confused with, the institution's more formal orientation activities. The program provides students with a chance to meet with other incoming students and learn about the traditions, rituals, and spirit of the University of Texas—clearly important information for future alumni. The program also serves a purpose by having students hear university administrators, faculty, and alumni speak about getting the most out of the university experience.

As the students arrive on campus, the residence hall move-in period provides another premium opportunity for alumni affairs to partner with student affairs in welcoming students to campus and assisting them with the transition process. As most student affairs professionals are acutely aware, the first couple of weeks on a college campus often determine if students will choose to remain at the institution and ultimately complete their degree. At Bellarmine University the alumni office provides each new student with a welcome kit. This is a packet that includes a key chain, phone card, and postcard, all featuring the university's seal. The idea is to make all incoming students feel that they belong at the institution from the moment they set foot on campus. At Arizona State University the alumni office provides lemonade to the students, their families, and the workers who help on move-in day. Though this seems like a relatively simple gesture, it goes a long way toward creating the kind of positive atmosphere needed to make students and their families feel good about the institution while moving large boxes into a small room in 90 degree weather. At Penn State, the alumni association provides each student with items from their "Be a Part, From the Start" collection of merchandise. This is a somewhat subtle though remarkably effective way of encouraging student participation in the institution's various alumni programs.

## Student Alumni Organizations

Traditionally, the most successful attempts to enhance the connection between students and alumni have involved the creation of organizations called student foundations and student alumni associations. They are a relatively inexpensive although very effective means of educating students about the institution and fostering interaction with alumni (Gaier, 2001). Not only do these student groups influence campus life positively, they are a wonderful way to identify and train future alumni leaders. Such associations view students philosophically as alumni-in-residence while they are enrolled at the institution. Most student alumni organizations follow one of three models, all of which are formally recognized by the Council for the Advancement and Support of Education (CASE) and its Association of Student Alumni Programs (ASAP). They are typically recognized student organizations and tend to operate under the auspices of alumni affairs offices.

**Service Organizations.** Many student alumni organizations are patterned after campus service organizations. The undergraduates serve as hosts and hostesses during alumni events, provide campus tours, assist with admissions recruitment activities, and sometimes provide assistance with routine tasks in the alumni office (folding and stuffing envelopes). At the University of Alabama, membership in the student alumni association is one of the most highly sought-after student leadership opportunities at the school. Prospective members are interviewed and selected by current members. Though it is a closed membership group, students and staff work to ensure that the members reflect the diversity of the campus. The organization sponsors social and fund-raising events, and each individual is asked to donate a specific number of community service hours each semester. Members support literacy instruction, blood drives, and food banks, and monies raised support an annual upperclassman scholarship chosen by the membership.

Other student alumni associations (SAA), based on the campus service model, coordinate parent or family weekends. During these weekends, SAA members have a significant role in coordinating events for the family members of the currently enrolled students. They also might simply serve as tour guides and ambassadors. Nuza (1998) and Brant (2000) also report that another SAA focus is the promotion and coordination of senior week or commencement activities. These events are hosted by the SAA in recognition and celebration of the senior class. They range from simple receptions to graduation fairs in which the senior students may register for commencement apparel, join the formal alumni organization, acquire short-term medical insurance, and order graduation announcements.

**Membership Organizations.** Another model of student alumni organizations permits students to enroll in their school's general alumni association. Like alumni, student members pay dues and receive the benefits of membership while enrolled. At the University of South Carolina, there are 2,300 active student members in the alumni organization. They receive the benefits of association membership, including discounts, a subscription to the alumni magazine, and the chance to support the alumni scholarship program. Membership organizations have the added benefit of providing current students with the chance to enhance their leadership skills. Students also learn more about the heritage of their institution and the accomplishments of its graduates by attending general alumni events, and they establish personal and professional contacts that may serve as resources while they are enrolled as well as after graduation.

**Student Foundations.** Some student alumni organizations are designed along the lines of the institutional advancement model. These organizations encourage student interest in the institution's fund-raising initiatives. They encourage modest donations through student giving and class gift programs and provide logistical support for the annual fund drive by soliciting alumni donations. One of the primary goals of this type of student alumni association involves learning how to accurately identify current students who may be inclined to be major institutional donors once they become alumni. Although fund-raising is obviously the main focus of this type of student organization, there is an important camaraderie that naturally occurs among the student members.

The Indiana University Student Foundation (IUSF), at the Bloomington campus, is organized around the student foundation model. It was founded in 1950, and currently has more than four hundred members operating under the direction of a twenty-five-member steering committee. The IUSF annually sponsors more than sixty events, including the annual Little 500 men's and women's bike race. These events raise significant funds for the association's scholarship program. At Georgia Tech, the student foundation coordinates its own annual fund campaign. According to Ryan (1992), the foundation members personally solicit their fellow students and encourage the other alumni-in-residence to make multiyear pledges to support class gifts and other initiatives. Ryan reports that 10 percent of the school's students contribute annually. The student foundation also manages its own endowment account and determines how to distribute the earnings from its investments to campus groups that apply for supporting grants. Involvement with the student foundation provides students with valuable educational experiences regarding fund management and investment options. The institution receives the long-term benefit in that student foundation participants, once they become alumni, become good annual fund volunteers. Ryan indicates that these participants also have a deeper understanding of the school's need for private support.

Regardless of their organizational structure, student alumni organizations exist to reinforce and support the historical educational experience provided by the institution. Their services and activities help to perpetuate institutional values from one generation to the next, which in turn tends to instill within alumni a deep sense of connectedness to the institution. It is this connectedness that generates positive alumni feelings about the institution and compels them to assist with future endeavors. Therefore, most colleges and universities find it extremely advantageous to invest heavily in their student alumni associations.

## Alumni and Career Development

An attribute often associated with career success is the identification of a mentor who will assist students in their transition from college to the work world. Alumni are particularly well-suited to the task. They are able to draw on their experiences in helping undergraduates explore the world of work, network, find jobs, and more. Indeed, there are several benefits to having alumni work closely with students, especially as they make their initial career decisions. Alumni are in a unique position to provide practical instruction and guidance to students who are majoring in disciplines that correlate with the careers of alumni. Along with the personal satisfaction that comes from contributing to the development of another person, the participating alumni are provided with an opportunity to observe students who might eventually be candidates for positions in their own organizations. A number of alumni organizations sponsor job-shadowing and mentoring programs, summer job placement, or internship opportunities for currently enrolled students, and help connect alumni employers with potential job candidates for their organizations.

**Mentoring Programs.** At Penn State, the LionLink program provides a networking service that connects Penn State students with alumni and other professionals in the student's chosen field of interest. Students and alumni career coaches register on-line to participate in the program. Students complete an on-line geographical and occupational profile and indicate their coach preferences. The LionLink coordinator uses this information to link a student with a coach. The student is responsible for making the first contact and scheduling the first meeting. Although the majority of these meetings are for information gathering, they also help the career seeker to make contacts in a selected profession. During the 2000–01 school year, 826 currently enrolled students registered as career seekers, and they had the opportunity to be in contact with 2,169 career coaches. Much of this mentoring takes place through electronic communications because the majority of the school's alumni do not reside near the campus.

Alumni associations for institutions located in metropolitan areas are in a fortunate position to facilitate direct contact between students and mentors throughout the academic year. At the University of Cincinnati, the alumni organization's Career Explorations program brings together alumni who reside in the greater metropolitan area with students interested in particular career fields. Volunteers and staff review applications from career explorers (students) and mentors (alumni) as well as conduct interviews with interested students to help determine which mentors and protégés make the best matches. Once the mentoring match assignments are made, the pairs are encouraged to meet in person two to four times throughout an academic year.

**Externship and Internship Opportunities.** Increasingly, students desire to complete some level of in-the-field training before they graduate from a particular degree program. Alumni often are in a good position for providing students with hands-on learning experiences in specific careers. Although some students are fortunate to be paid during their time of service as a company or organization intern, many students participate simply for the benefits of the experience. At Miami University in Oxford, Ohio, students participate in a one- to two-week on-site career externship in which a currently enrolled student is paired with a Miami graduate working in the student's career field of interest. The program tries to identify externships in a geographic location that is also of interest to the students. The students are responsible for their own housing, meals, and transportation expenses during their externship, but they also have the opportunity to network with their alumni sponsor and to gain practical experience through the course of their visit.

At Illinois State University, students identify internship and cooperative education opportunities, frequently offered by alumni employers, through the school's Student and Alumni Placement Services program. Employers work with placement coordinators to establish for-credit professional practice courses that provide students with career experience, academic credit, and professional guidance. The institution makes a distinction between internships and cooperative educational experiences. Internships are defined as those educational opportunities that a student has near the end of the collegiate career in which the sum of previous instruction in the field may be applied. Cooperative education experiences are those that students may participate in during any period of their collegiate education, and the focus is more toward learning about a field than in refining their skills in a particular career.

**Job Placement Programs.** A number of alumni associations, in concert with university career services operations, also provide information on job placement opportunities for soon-to-be-graduates and alumni. At Georgia State University both students and alumni make use of on-line job recruitment and search systems (such as MonsterTRAK.com). These systems provide job seekers with access to a searchable database of national and international positions. They also allow employers to selectively review electronic resumés based on keyword searches that match candidate skills with job requirements. Although many institutions provide these services for free to current students, the majority of programs servicing alumni either require membership in the alumni association or payment of an additional fee for graduates to utilize these resources.

Alumni make excellent career counselors because they provide valuable insights into the political and cultural dimensions associated with various professions, industries, and individual companies. Career-related programs offer other benefits to students and alumni. Students receive professional guidance from their mentors, including advice about career paths and advancement strategies from internship supervisors. These programs are highly praised by students who seek to hone their skills in real-world settings and to increase their self-confidence. The students develop important networking and professional contacts, as well as an employment history, to draw on when they are ready to seek full-time employment.

## Campus Programming

Alumni organizations, often in conjunction with student affairs offices, increasingly are engaged in developing programming and activities for currently enrolled students. Many colleges have a single student and alumni committee that plans the annual homecoming celebration. Other institutions provide specific transition programs for entering students or graduating seniors. Still others bring students and alumni together by providing service to the communities in which the institutions are located. These opportunities provide colleges and universities with ways of involving alumni in the lives of students throughout the school year.

**Homecoming.** On a majority of campuses, homecoming is the quintessential student and alumni event. While the term *homecoming* generally implies that this is the official time for alumni to return "home" to their alma mater after moving on to other phases of their lives, homecoming may foster more involvement among current students than among past graduates. Almost every college and university sponsors an annual homecoming festival; for many institutions it is the major programming opportunity of the school year. Student and alumni organizations alike host some of their most widely publicized and heavily financed activities during this period, which typically lasts about a week and tends to culminate with a major sports event. Homecoming often serves as the model for all collaborative ventures between student affairs and alumni affairs; it is the one occasion that seems to inspire both divisions to freely and selflessly cooperate for the greater good of the institution, its current students, and its alumni.

In many ways the currently enrolled students add much of the color and flair to the homecoming celebration. The event is a great opportunity to have alumni assist students in the continuation of campus traditions—from providing guidance on float construction to planning for other events on campus. Students should be full participants in the homecoming celebration because their student homecoming experience, as an attendee at a bonfire or as a member of the marching band, will influence the decision to return to campus to experience homecoming traditions as alumni (McDaniel, 2000).

Although some institutions hold separate events for students and alumni, the occasions that bring all members of the campus community together are most special. If a school holds a pregame celebration on homecoming day, the alumni office may arrange to have the members of the current student spirit and musical groups perform. Alumni enjoy having contact with currently enrolled students. In order to foster student and alumni contact at Georgia Tech, alumni are invited to adopt a student for a day during homecoming (Scalzo, 1994). Students are matched with alumni based either on shared academic major or by hometown. Students escort the alumni during their visit to campus and help reacquaint them with the institution. Alumni and students attend classes, take tours of the campus, and together discover past and current favorite faculty, places, and memories. Although the program provides students with the benefit of networking with alumni, it also provides alumni with the benefit of feeling closer to, and more knowledgeable about, the institution.

There are other methods of connecting current and former students during homecoming. One approach is by holding reunions for former involved students (campus leaders, cheerleaders, band members) in conjunction with their homecoming celebrations. These reunions allow the current members of those groups to interact with their alumni. These reunions also serve to help educate the former student leaders about the needs of student groups and help to develop alumni interest in supporting student organizations financially. Another strategy is to include prospective students in major homecoming activities. Because homecoming events provide a good opportunity to showcase the best of a college or university, alumni associations should consider partnering with admissions offices to include prospective students (alumni of the future) in these events as well.

**Transition Programs.** Alumni-sponsored transition programs for students may range from the traditional summer orientation to the more formal capstone seminar. Such programs are designed to better connect students with the campus and to help them better understand their eventual role as alumni. Some of these programs are primarily social or celebratory in nature. The alumni office at Carnegie Mellon University, for example, coordinates a Dinner with Twelve Strangers program. These dinner parties connect six students, three alumni, and three professors from a particular college or school of the university. The dinners are free and open to students, and the topics of discussion range from the modern curriculum to the changes in student life through the years.

Another transition program is the annual senior ring ceremony. This event is one of the ways in which an institution conveys to its future alumni that they are members of a select community—the alumni of the school—who may be identified by the common symbol of the class ring. At Vanderbilt University the alumni association and the student affairs office coordinate the annual parents weekend and hold the ring ceremony as part of this weekend. All students who have purchased the school's official ring, as well as their families, are invited to attend the formal presentation. The alumni association president presents each student with his or her ring. At the conclusion of the ceremony, students are asked to place the ring on their finger and raise their hand in celebration of reaching this milestone.

While some alumni organizations host social activities for students, others coordinate programs that are more instructional in nature. At Carnegie Mellon University, the Robert G. McCurdy Slice of Life program is a Saturday conference for exiting graduates focusing on a variety of post-college issues. Topics range from career development to financial management to personal relationships. Alumni of the university present the interest sessions and the alumni office coordinates the program with other units on campus. Similarly, at the University of North Carolina–Chapel Hill the university's general alumni association has established a series of personal development programs to offer to currently enrolled students. This alumni organization offers the student members of the alumni association courses in self-defense, credit management, Internet resources, and time management. Both of these programs are designed to help the alumni-in-residence successfully manage the life transitions of the collegiate experience.

**Community Service Programs.** Alumni and students can be brought together in other formal programs. Community service projects are a particularly effective means of precipitating meaningful interaction between students and alumni. The underlying principle behind all service learning programs is the idea that there are more important considerations in life than just taking care of our own individual interests and ourselves. Community service programs can precipitate an interaction between students and alumni that has the potential to impart significant institutional values. At the University of Louisville in Kentucky, for instance, the student organization for alumni relations and the alumni association board of directors coordinate an annual "repair affair day" with a local housing foundation. During this activity, teams of volunteers composed of students and alumni make repairs and improvements to several houses in the campus neighborhood. At the University of Southern Indiana, the student alumni organization sponsors an annual holiday tree-lighting event. Students, alumni, family, and friends gather together to witness the annual lighting of the association's tree and enjoy the campus singers. Admission to the event is a nonperishable food item, which is given to a local food bank.

According to Scalzo (1994), the University of Notre Dame in Indiana has had a formal alumni community service program since 1990. The program connects students and alumni in volunteer service. In conjunction with the university's Center for Social Concerns, students and alumni work together in cleanup efforts and other projects. Scalzo reports that in 1993, for example, participants spent a week working in an area of St. Louis that had suffered flooding and where many of the school's alumni resided. Staff from the alumni office found the event to be successful in making students aware of ways in which individuals can manage their full-time jobs and still provide public service. It also made alumni aware of the idealism and energy of the students. In addition, these types of activities help create positive public relations exposure for the sponsoring institution.

## Other Initiatives

Although alumni associations primarily play a role in student life through assisting with the admissions process, sponsoring student alumni organizations, enhancing career education, and developing campus programs, there are other activities through which alumni offices support student life and education. Alumni might be invited to support students who are continuing their education through an exchange program. In addition, alumni can be asked to serve as faculty members in order to bring discussions of real-life applications of the principles of a discipline into the classroom.

**Hosting Visiting Students.**  Alumni organizations are in a good position to assist students who venture from their home campuses to study at other institutions through study-abroad or exchange programs. At the University of Louisville the alumni office works with the student life office to connect students participating in the National Student Exchange (NSE) with alumni in the area of their exchange school. The university's regional alumni clubs invite the visiting student to local events and individual club members ask students to share the occasional meal. Moreover, after having contact with these NSE students, a number of the regional alumni clubs provide scholarship assistance to them.

**Alumni in the Classroom.**  Scalzo (1994) notes a program coordinated by the alumni and career development offices at Muhlenberg College in Pennsylvania in which more than forty alumni return to campus to lecture as part of the established curriculum. The sponsoring offices survey professors to determine which of them are willing to have an alumnus/a address their classes. Based on faculty interest, alumni are identified and invited as guest faculty to lecture, participate in panel discussions, and give interviews to students. The coordinators of this program indicate that one of its greatest benefits is that students have a chance to learn about the careers of liberal arts graduates (for example, how a language major can work for a trucking company). Students also report the benefit of learning about career paths and emerging trends in various fields. This type of program provides a positive learning experience for the students as well as reconnects alumni with their alma mater.

## Benefits of Collaboration with Alumni Associations

Students who are engaged in campus life are more likely to feel a stronger connection to the school once they become alumni. They are more inclined to assist in promoting the institution through participation in various efforts aimed at recruiting new students. Moreover, alumni who were members of major student organizations while in college tend to give back more to the institution after graduation than do their less involved counterparts (Conley, 1999). Jablonski (2000) notes that alumni professionals need to understand the current student experience so that they can plan programs and services for the future as well connect with these students while they are enrolled. This becomes important because alumni financial support increasingly is critical to state-assisted colleges and universities as government funding decreases and costs continue to escalate. Gaier (2001) studied the role of alumni in the financial support of higher education and found that alumni who are financial contributors are more likely to be involved with their alma maters in other ways.

Partnerships between student and alumni affairs afford their institutions extraordinary advantages. They provide opportunities for students to observe and model the behavior and actions of involved alumni—behavior that includes assisting students and the institution with time, advice, and financial support. In turn, these opportunities help the alumni-in-residence to develop a greater understanding of what the institution expects of him or her after graduation. Students involved in these programs have a unique chance to get to know potential colleagues and employers.

Alumni organizations also provide students with involvement opportunities that enhance their leadership skills by giving them the chance to interact with significant social and professional contacts. Such networking and professional contacts are invaluable to students. Student alumni programs also offer opportunities for out-of-class learning experiences. Membership in student alumni organizations is considered an honor at many campuses.

For alumni who are involved with student associations and programs, the benefits are similar. Alumni play an important role in supporting student organizations and their activities. In many cases, student organizations, particularly fraternal organizations, have advisory boards composed primarily of alumni. Their meaningful contacts with current students facilitate their connection to the daily life of their alma mater. These experiences with students, particularly with students studying in their own discipline, often serve to validate the worth of their own degrees and credentials. The provision of scholarships is another significant contribution that alumni make, both collectively and individually. Their financial support makes college a reality for many students. Finally, through career-related programs, alumni have the opportunity to identify potential employees and colleagues.

## Conclusion

It is important to note that the partnerships facilitated between student and alumni programs have benefits for sponsoring institutions. These programs provide opportunities to expose currently enrolled students to the behavior and actions of involved alumni. These modeled behaviors by current alumni (assisting students and the institution with time, advice, and financial support) may help the alumni-in-residence develop an understanding of institutional expectations for its graduates. In addition, the more that colleges and universities are able to connect alumni with currently enrolled students, the better alumni will understand why the institution asks for financial support. Student alumni programs help give a human face to scholarships and other campus programs needing private support.

Student alumni programs always should reinforce the institution's educational values that have endured over time, values that alumni help pass on to students from one generation to the next. Whenever alumni and students have the occasion to interact, both groups, as well as the institution they have in common, tend to benefit significantly. These interactions provide participants with opportunities for interpersonal and professional growth and development. The colleges and universities that are able to link their alumni with current students enhance their reputations as quality educational institutions. The understanding of the need for private support is increased through these efforts. For these reasons, institutions are well-advised to consider developing and investing in partnership opportunities that connect alumni with student life.

## References

Brant, K. E. "Student Alumni Associations: Student Involvement in the Alumni Profession." In J. A. Feudo (ed.), *Alumni Relations: A Newcomer's Guide to Success.* New York: Council for the Advancement and Support of Education, 2000.

Conley, A. "Student Organization Membership and Alumni Giving at a Public, Research University." Unpublished doctoral dissertation, School of Education, Indiana University, 1999.

Dolbert, S. C. "Alumni admissions programs." In J. A. Feudo (ed.), *Alumni Relations: A Newcomer's Guide to Success.* New York: Council for the Advancement and Support of Education, 2000.

Gaier, S. *Increasing Alumni Involvement and Alumni Financial Support Through a Student Alumni Association.* Washington, D.C.: ERIC Clearinghouse on Higher Education, 2001. (ED 451 767)

Garland, P., and Grace, T. *New Perspectives for Student Affairs Professionals: Evolving Realities, Responsibilities and Roles.* Washington, D.C.: George Washington University, ERIC Clearinghouse on Higher Education, 1994. (ED 370 507)

Hanson, S. "Alumni Characteristics that Predict Promoting and Donating to Alma Mater: Implications for Alumni Relations." Unpublished doctoral dissertation, Department of Educational Foundations and Research, University of North Dakota, 2000.

Jablonski, M. R. "Collaborations Between Student Affairs and Alumni Relations." In J. A. Feudo (ed.), *Alumni Relations: A Newcomer's Guide to Success.* New York: Council for the Advancement and Support of Education, 2000.

Kellogg, K. "An Analysis of the Collaborative Programming Between Student Affairs and Alumni Relations Professionals at Select Post-Secondary Institutions in Missouri." Unpublished doctoral dissertation, Graduate School, University of Missouri–Columbia, 1996.

McDaniel, S. M. "Homecoming." In J. A. Feudo (ed.), *Alumni Relations: A Newcomer's Guide to Success.* New York: Council for the Advancement and Support of Education, 2000.

Nuza, J. "A Powerful Network." *CASE Currents,* 1998, 24(6), 12–13.

Ryan, E. "Foundations for the Future." *CASE Currents,* 1992, 18(3), 24–27.

Scalzo, T. "United Efforts: A Look at Five Campus Programs that Bring Students and Alumni Together." *CASE Currents,* 1994, 20(9), 35–39.

*TARA S. SINGER is the former assistant vice president for alumni relations and the current director of regional leadership gifts at the University of Louisville.*

*AARON W. HUGHEY is professor of counseling and student affairs in the College of Education and Behavioral Science at Western Kentucky University.*

**6**

*This chapter reviews how and why career services have changed since the 1970s and identifies some ways to effectively utilize employers to enhance the student experience and strengthen institutional relationships.*

# The Emergence of Career Services and Their Important Role in Working with Employers

*Gary L. McGrath*

Career services have emerged over the last thirty years to become a more visible and vital part of student affairs on college campuses. In response to student concerns about their job prospects following graduation, career services have offered more comprehensive assistance to students and serve as the institution's primary contact for employers interested in hiring its graduates. Recognizing the need for students to be clear in their career goals in order to conduct an effective job search, career services have offered more in the way of career counseling and opportunities to interact with employers prior to interviewing for a job. The emphasis on career counseling and programming has attracted practitioners with advanced degrees in counseling and student affairs. Although career services are at times located in the various colleges of large universities and report to a college dean or associate dean, the majority of career service operations, particularly those that are centralized, report to student affairs (Nagle and Bohovich, 2000).

The opportunity for career services to serve as the institution's liaison with employers can be a valuable resource for students, faculty, and staff. Simultaneously, career services can be subject to unrealistic expectations on the part of students, parents, college administrators, and employers. The purpose of this chapter is to review how and why career services have changed and identify some effective ways to utilize employers to enhance the student experience and strengthen institutional relationships.

NEW DIRECTIONS FOR STUDENT SERVICES, no. 100, Winter 2002  © Wiley Periodicals, Inc.

## Transformation of Career Services

During the 1970s campus placement offices underwent an extensive transformation from offices with limited functions—relatively invisible on campus—to comprehensive career services attracting the attention of students and the news media. Previously placement offices or placement bureaus could be characterized as often having few staff located in poor facilities away from the center of campus activities. These low-profile offices were a place where seniors seeking employment would visit to establish a credential file in case they might need letters of recommendation for employment, perhaps sign up for interviews with employers visiting the campus, or review job vacancy listings.

Significant changes in the job market and higher education enrollments during the early 1970s prompted universities and even liberal arts colleges to reassess and offer more career assistance to their students. Until that time students and their parents had been relatively confident that earning a college degree, any four-year college degree, was a credential that almost assured the holder of a good job with commensurate compensation. The combination of slower economic growth and a dramatic increase in the number of college graduates challenged these assumptions. Approximately eight million college graduates entered the workforce between 1969 to 1976 compared to four million from 1962 to 1969 (Hecker, 1978, p. 37). "Overall it is estimated that one out of four graduates of the 1970s experienced a higher rate of unemployment and underemployment than their predecessors" (p. 37). With a large number of college graduates to choose from, employers attempted to reduce the number of applications by requiring candidates to have degrees and work experience that seemed directly related to the available openings. Contributing to the woes of college graduates seeking employment was a more competitive job market for those seeking elementary and secondary education teaching positions. Education graduates, not able to find teaching positions, were now competing with other graduates for business and government positions (McGrath, 1981). Students responded to this concern about their employment prospects by choosing college degrees in fields such as business, which they assumed would make them more attractive to employers.

After unprecedented growth in college enrollments during the 1960s, higher education in the 1970s began to experience stable or declining enrollments. Colleges and universities now were faced with competing for students and became more concerned about retaining students. Prospective students and their parents and, in some cases, state legislators began asking questions about what percentage of graduates by discipline found employment after graduation and what kind of career assistance was available to students. In some cases the career services staff were asked to participate in prospective student recruiting programs. To improve student retention, college and university officials began to acknowledge the need to assist students with identifying a sense of career direction as illustrated by the following statement from an academic dean: "Five years ago this writer greeted freshmen and their parents during summer orientation with the following statement: 'It's not our responsibility to get you jobs. Our responsibility is to provide for you to have a creative learning experience.' Three years later I said, 'Not only do we assume it to be our responsibility to assist you in setting career objectives, but here are the programs that we have designed to accomplish this" (Rose, 1978, p. 62). The interest in attracting and retaining students contributed to higher education recognizing the need to provide more career assistance to their students.

## Continued Concern and Change

Students and parents continued to be concerned about the employment and salary prospects of college graduates throughout the 1980s and 1990s as the job market fluctuated. Although the job market has generally been good for recent college graduates during the last few years, the cost of tuition at public and private colleges and universities has risen dramatically along with student loan debt, contributing to the concern among students and parents about the economic benefits of a college education. At the beginning of the twenty-first century the economy has entered a recession resulting in, again, a very competitive job market for college graduates.

Over the last two and a half decades career services has emphasized certain core activities, responded to the interest of students in gaining work experience in their chosen profession prior to graduation, and eliminated some services that are no longer necessary. In a survey of career offices conducted in December 1999 and January 2000 the following services were most frequently offered: career counseling (93.1 percent), occupational and employer information library (91.8 percent), placement of graduates in full-time employment (90.8 percent), and campus interviewing (88.1 percent). There was a significant increase in the number of career services offering cooperative education, internship, and experiential education over the last twenty-five years, from 26 percent in 1975 to 78.3 percent in 2000. One of the few services to decline was credential services, from 79 percent in 1975 to 52.8 percent in 2000 (Nagle and Bohovich, 2000). The increase in the percentage of career services offering opportunities for undergraduate students to participate in structured learning and working arrangements reflects the interest of students gaining experience in their chosen career fields. As fewer business employers requested written letters of recommendations, there was less need to maintain credential files.

Technology has been extensively incorporated into career services operations and by employers recruiting students. Career counselors use computer software to help students in self-assessment and career information searches. Students now conduct the preponderance of their research on employers electronically, and employers have recognized the importance of attractive and informative web sites. The management of the entire campus recruiting process is handled electronically. Some employers require all applications for employment to be submitted on-line. Although technology has made it easier for students to communicate with employers, it has also required a significant investment on the part of career services in terms of equipment and staff with technical expertise (Nagle and Bohovich, 2000).

## Reconciling Expectations of Career Services

As career offices have become more visible and offered a broader array of services, they continue to face the challenge of reconciling the different expectations of students, employers, campus administrators, and faculty. In spite of their expressing concern about finding suitable employment following graduation, students often do not invest much time or effort in identifying their interests and investigating various occupational options. Students often delay starting their job search until just before or even after graduation, long after many employers have completed their hiring. Frequently employers do not realize the planning and effort required to effectively recruit college graduates. Employers may not anticipate their hiring needs early enough to participate in campus interviews and many have unrealistic expectations of student interest in the positions they have available.

Campus administrators and faculty often are not familiar with what their career services do, and they are sometimes unrealistic about what can be accomplished. While administrators and faculty want to hear about the success of graduates, they also need to provide the resources and support for career services to do their job. Employers form opinions of an institution based on their experience when visiting the campus and their previous success in hiring students at that institution. From the employers' perspective, did they interview students with the qualifications they were seeking? Were the students prepared for the interview and seem genuinely interested in the positions available and the company? Did the career services staff handle the arrangements for the interview promptly and competently? Were faculty or other campus administrators willing to meet with employers?

Is career services located in a reasonably visible location with functional campus interview accommodations? Something as seemingly minor as access to convenient parking on a campus, particularly an urban campus, can be a significant issue with some employers. Effective campus interviewing programs require a great deal of planning and attention to detail on the part of the career services staff along with the technical resources and facilities to be successful.

Sometimes administrators and faculty make the career services office the scapegoat for student dissatisfaction with their employment prospects. For career services staff to be effective in helping students, they need the cooperation, support, and understanding of campus administrators and faculty.

It is not unusual for the campus development office to seek out the career services director for help in identifying and soliciting employers for donations. This is fairly common at colleges and universities where there is fierce competition among employers for graduates in technical areas such as engineering and computer science. The assumption is that if an employer has been successful in hiring a number of the institution's graduates, they would be candidates for a financial contribution. The career services director needs to make it clear to the development officer that all employers, even those who do not make a donation, will have equal access to outstanding students. The problem is that career services can be perceived by other competing employers as favoring one company over the other because of the donation. The risk is "the danger of offending many employers to benefit a few" (Stewart, 1993, p. 47).

Career services operating budgets, like so many areas in higher education, may be inadequate to provide the kinds of quality services and programs desired. Senior student affairs officers sometimes believe career services can generate additional revenue by charging students and employers fees for particular services. For example, for many years it was common for students to be charged a fee to establish a placement or credential file with the career services office. The rationale was to recover the cost of printing attractive cover folders, copying, and mailing credential files with references to employers. As fewer employers requested credential files it became more difficult to rationalize charging students a fee to establish a file that might never be requested. Some career services required students to pay an office registration fee to participate in campus interviews and access job vacancies. Career services registration fees became an obstacle for students who were skeptical about the value of using career services and an irritation to students who thought assistance with something as basic as trying to find a job after graduation should not be assessed a fee.

The practice of career services charging employers fees to recover the costs of room rentals, parking, food, and publicity to participate in programs such as job fairs is accepted practice. At institutions where graduates have been in heavy demand for employment the last few years, there is the temptation during times of tight career-services budgets to charge employers fees in return for priority access to students. A lean operating budget "has provided many career centers with the opportunity and expectation of bringing in money that their predecessors a decade ago would never have imagined"(Goodman, Rayman, and Ferrell, 2001, p. 22). Career services directors and their supervisors carefully need to consider the implications of what fees are appropriate and justified. As one employer commented, "Access is not something we should buy" (Goodman, Rayman, and Ferrell, 2001, p. 27).

It is also worth remembering that the job market for graduates, particularly technical graduates, can change rapidly. Although there will be periods when there is fierce competition among employers for college graduates in particular fields, in other years employers will choose not to recruit on campus or will limit recruiting in response to a less robust economy. In strong and weak recruiting years career services need to maintain good working relationships with all the employers interested in their graduates. The National Association of Colleges and Employers (NACE) "Principles for Professional Conduct" states, "Career services professionals will provide generally comparable services to all employers, regardless of whether the employers contribute services, gifts, or financial support to the educational institution or office and regardless of the level of such support" (NACE, p. 4). Gifts from employers can help furnish career offices, provide up-to-date technical equipment, and support a variety of programs to assist students. Campus administrators, including the development office and career services, need to be clear to employers making donations under what conditions gifts can be accepted.

Along with the greater visibility career services has received comes a variety of sometimes competing expectations and demands from campus officials, students, and employers. The career services director needs to thoughtfully articulate what can be realistically accomplished and under what circumstances at that particular institution to those various constituents.

## The Relationship of Career Services with Employers

The career services office has a unique and important role in linking students with employers. The best contacts with employers are of little help to students who are not clear about what they want to do after graduation. Help with basic career concerns—such as identifying interests, values, and skills—how to research possible occupational interests, teaching resumé writing, and how to prepare for employment interviews are a very important foundation for career counselors offering help to undergraduates. As the NACE survey illustrated, career counseling has been the most frequently offered career office service since 1981 (Nagle and Bohovich, 2000). Employers can be a valuable resource to career services staff offering career counseling. The knowledge and understanding gained from interaction with employers adds reality and credibility to career services staff when assisting students with career concerns. A number of ways are available to employers so that they can be more visible on campus and enhance the career development of students. Selected strategies follow.

**On-Campus Interviewing.** On-campus interviewing is a very common, popular, and expected function of college and university career services. Large national organizations and local employers have used on-campus interviews as a way to hire entry-level professionals for decades. Particularly for some academic majors, such as accounting, computer science, and engineering, on-campus interviews typically generate many job offers to the seniors in those programs. Students like and, in many cases, expect the opportunity to interview on campus because campus recruiting provides a convenient way for them to meet with prospective employers. Students can arrange on-campus interviews to minimize missing classes, and employers have access to a number of interested and presumably qualified candidates for employment. The career services office is perceived as serving the "matchmaker" function. "The goal of having the right student in the right room with the right employer at the right time seems straightforward and perhaps simple to accomplish" (Stewart, 1993, p. 41). However, campus recruiting is not as easy or as simple as it seems.

Employers increasingly have become more selective in where they recruit. Decisions often are based on the employer's history of attracting candidates who match their selection criteria and being successful in hiring those to whom they make offers. By choosing a few colleges and universities, many employers feel they can concentrate their efforts on attracting the students who best match their particular profile of a successful employee. The pressure is on career services to deliver students who meet the criteria of the employer. Requiring a certain major and high grade-point average often is used as a way to limit the number of students eligible to interview. Employers expect to review resumés in advance and select the students they will invite to be interviewed. Career services staff regularly face the challenge of trying to provide interview opportunities for the many students who may not fit the employer's standard hiring criteria. For example, employers may want to limit on-campus interviews to students with a particular major, an excellent grade-point average, and some evidence of related experience through part-time work or an internship. Students with a modest grade-point average and little in the way of work experience or participation in campus organizations and activities may have a difficult time being selected for interviews. On-campus interviewing also presumes that employers will know their exact hiring needs months in advance and that students will be prepared early in their senior year to commit to a specific position with a particular organization.

Career services staff face many challenges in working with employers seeking to interview on campus. Sometimes employers are ineffective in providing information describing the positions to be filled and the qualifications desired of candidates. Companies may send poorly prepared personnel to conduct on-campus interviews. Some employers are slow in informing candidates of their status after campus interviews. This is particularly frustrating to students who are trying to decide among job offers with strict time deadlines. Employers who are successful in interviewing on campus tend to be those who are willing to make a consistent effort over a number of years and follow through on their commitments. Successful employers enjoy being on college campuses; they relate well to students and the career services staff. They are knowledgeable about their organization and realistic about what to expect of students when interviewing on campus.

It is very difficult for small liberal arts colleges and smaller regional universities, often located in rural areas, to attract a large pool of employers interested in interviewing on campus. Although these kinds of institutions have some outstanding students, they simply do not have the critical number of students to warrant the time and effort of large national employers to interview on campus. It is understandable that of the colleges and universities responding to the NACE survey of career services, the average percentage of graduating seniors who obtained their jobs through on-campus interviewing was only 23 percent (Nagle and Bohovich, 2000).

**Cooperative Education and Internships.** Many students seek the opportunity to gain work experience in their chosen fields prior to graduation. Teacher education programs have been leaders in providing this kind of valuable exposure to teaching at the elementary and secondary level as part of their curriculum. Cooperative education programs, where students are supervised by a faculty member, and alternately working and attending classes over many terms, have been in existence since early in the twentieth century. Institutions such as the University of Cincinnati, Northeastern University, University of Detroit, Rochester Institute of Technology, Georgia Technological University, and the University of Akron were early leaders in cooperative education. These institutions recognized the value of providing opportunities for engineering students to apply what they were learning in the classroom off campus (Barbeau, 1985). For cooperative education to work, it requires a significant commitment on the part of faculty in planning their curricular offerings to coincide with off-campus work experiences.

In contrast, internships generally occur for a fixed period of time, such as an academic term or summer, during which the student works with an employer. Sometimes the internship is a specific project agreed upon in advance with the employer and student. If academic credit is arranged, a faculty member establishes the learning goals and appropriate assignments that must be completed. Internships can be paid or unpaid depending on a number of factors including whether the placement is with a profit or nonprofit organization and what the demand is for graduates in that particular field. Increasingly popular with students, internships have become a positive factor in enhancing the student's job prospects after graduation.

A number of potential benefits of internships accrue to students, employers, and faculty members. Students have an opportunity to determine if their perceptions of working in an area of interest and with a particular company are compatible. By working with a knowledgeable practitioner, they learn about the nature of professional work. Shapero (1985) has described professional work as "unspecifiable, it is dependent on situation and problem, and requires judgment, ingenuity, and creativity of an individual possessing a particular body of knowledge" (p. xvi). Students learn the often ambiguous nature of assignments and responsibilities of professional work from internships. Under ideal conditions, students observe and experience the importance of eliciting the cooperation of others to complete tasks, the need to make decisions under time constraints and with less than complete information, and the ability to balance the priorities of multiple tasks (McGrath, 1985). Students have an opportunity to determine if the organization where they are doing their internship provides the kind of environment in which they would like to work after graduation. Sometimes the completion of a successful internship results in the student being offered a position by the organization with which they interned after graduation.

Employers appreciate the opportunity to observe a student over a longer period than it takes to conduct an interview to decide if the student should be considered for a future full-time position. Depending on how the student has performed during the internship, the employer can encourage or gently discourage the intern to seek employment after graduation with their organization. From the perspective of some employers, internships are a means to commit outstanding candidates to their organization before campus interviews in their senior year.

For faculty who supervise internships, the experience can provide valuable insight into how their academic discipline can be applied to particular projects within a nonacademic organization. As with nearly all aspects of employer relations, identifying, establishing, and maintaining appropriate internship sites with employers that meet the expectations of students and faculty is very time-consuming. Students need to plan carefully and thoughtfully identify their learning objectives with a faculty member. These learning objectives need to be understood and agreed upon by the on-site internship employer. Once the student arrives at the internship site, there should be some visits by the faculty member and the campus official supervising internships to ensure that the expectations of the student, employer, and faculty member are being met. If there are problems or concerns during the internship, someone from the campus needs to be available to identify a solution. Faculty may be unwilling to invest time in working with student interns unless the institution acknowledges these kinds of efforts when reviewing workloads, salary increases, or promotion decisions.

**Career and Job Fairs.** Career and job fairs are another way career services and employers can work together to their mutual benefit. Career fairs generally are characterized as events open to freshmen through seniors as a way for students to find out more about various employment opportunities. The purpose is for employers to provide career information rather than seeking to find candidates for current openings. Practicing professionals who agree to participate in career fairs are representing their profession, not necessarily their employer. Job fairs, on the other hand, are targeted for seniors interested in seeking employment. Hosting career or job fairs on campus is a good way to raise the visibility of career services to students and employers. Employers who have little name recognition among students can benefit by participating in these events. Fees charged to employers participating in the job fair can be pooled and used to generate publicity for the event. Some students who have not been aware of the career services office may be attracted to attend the festival-like atmosphere of a job fair held in a visible location on campus, such as the campus union ballroom, and learn more about potential employers in a less formal format.

Job fairs can be particularly helpful to small liberal arts colleges and regional universities that often have a difficult time attracting employers to interview on campus. Employers may not feel they will see enough qualified candidates to merit their taking the time to interview on each of these campuses. A cooperatively sponsored job fair at a centrally located site can provide students access to employers who would not normally visit their campus.

Job fairs require a great deal of time, effort, and planning to be successful. Students are not likely to attend unless they believe the employers attending will offer positions of interest to them. Employers are not interested in staffing a table or booth for hours unless they believe a number of qualified students interested in their positions and company will visit them.

Both job fairs and career fairs also can be used by career services to sponsor workshops using a combination of career office staff and employers attending the event as speakers. It is important for the organizers of the career fair to be clear on what they are trying to accomplish. If the career fair is meant simply to give students an opportunity to gain some basic understanding of what job opportunities are available and what employers expect of candidates, that needs to be explained to students and employers attending the event. If the job fair is intended to provide opportunities for students to seek internships and full-time positions, students need to understand the importance of being prepared to dress appropriately, bring resumés if they have not been submitted in advance, and answer questions about themselves and why they are interested in that particular position and employer.

Student professional organizations frequently are interested in sponsoring employer career and job fairs for their respective academic program. The energy and enthusiasm student groups bring to these events can contribute to increasing student attendance. As students often underestimate the amount of lead time needed to plan these kinds of programs, the involvement of someone from career services is critical to ensure that appropriate contacts are made with employers and that planning is done well in advance.

Student organizations representing small and specialized degree programs may not have the critical number of interested students to warrant employers attending a career fair. These specialized groups might consider, as an alternative to a career fair, working with career services and faculty in their academic programs to offer a series of speakers from companies in the area. With the cooperation of faculty, employers could be invited to speak to classes. Career services might also consider arranging for a group of interested students to visit employers. Working with career services and the alumni office, faculty and student leaders also may identify alumni who are pleased to be offered the opportunity to speak on campus or arrange student visits to their organizations. Again, for these kinds of programs to be effective, a great deal of cooperation and planning between student leaders and career services is required.

**Information Interviewing, Shadowing, and Mentoring.** Students who have at least tentatively identified a possible career interest can benefit immensely from meeting people in that profession. Career services can facilitate these kinds of interactions, ranging from one-time information interviews lasting an hour to "shadowing" the professional through a workday to more formal interactions in which a professional serves as a mentor to a student, periodically meeting with him or her over the semester or academic year.

Career services can identify graduate and employer volunteers in the area who are willing to be interviewed by students interested in learning more about their professions. To do the interview correctly, the students will have completed some background reading about the profession and the company before arranging an appointment, preferably at the professional's place of business. By meeting at the employment site, students have an opportunity to see the workplace and envision whether they could work in that setting. They should be prepared with questions about how the person being interviewed entered the profession, his or her education and work experience, entry-level position titles, and what the employer looks for in new hires. The primary purpose of the visit is to help students determine if they would enjoy the actual day-to-day activities involved in doing the job and to gain insight into the appealing and less appealing aspects of the work. Students should consider interviewing at least one other person, perhaps at another organization, for the purpose of comparison.

Students spending a day or more with a professional in their field of interest provides them with the opportunity to observe the kinds of issues, problems, and interactions that are part of doing that particular kind of work. This kind of shadowing experience demystifies the nature of the work and helps students evaluate their continuing commitment to that occupation.

Mentoring programs usually involve linking a student with a professional and structuring a series of activities over a period of many months to help students and their mentors reflect on what is being learned. For example, the University of Florida Career Resource Center recently initiated a minority career mentoring program called Gator Launch. The yearlong program matches sophomores and first-semester juniors with professionals and requires participation in a series of regularly scheduled career seminars. Students are expected to meet with their mentors at least once a month and keep a log of these discussions. The career seminars occur once every two weeks with a heavy emphasis on self-assessment. The mentoring program is intended to help students consider how to connect their academic interests to a career. Students are also encouraged to consider planning internships after completing the program (*Gator Launch,* 2001).

**Involving Employers to Enhance Academic Advising.** There are many different ways academic advising is organized at colleges and universities. The responsibility for academic advising frequently is divided among professional staff and faculty. Whether it is faculty, professional staff, or graduate students, whoever actually does the academic advising can be a tremendous help to students with career concerns. Academic advisers have the opportunity to meet with freshmen and sophomores when they are trying to decide on their academic and career interests. If faculty are advising students, they may also have frequent contact with students by having advisees in their classes. Faculty contact with students early in their college careers, and on a regular basis, is in contrast to contacts by career services staff, who may not see students until their senior year, when it is too late to discuss internships or other career-enhancing opportunities. If academic advisers are familiar with some basic information about careers, they can help students avoid choosing a major simply based on assumptions about the career prospects of graduates with that degree.

Many academic advisers, including faculty, however, are not comfortable discussing career concerns with their advisees because they are often not familiar with the kinds of career opportunities currently available to their students. Following are two examples of how career services worked with advisory committees to link faculty with employers.

At the University of Minnesota the Faculty Advisory Committee of the College of Liberal Arts Career Development Office decided there was a need to enhance faculty involvement in advising undergraduates about careers and suggested arranging a meeting with employers. The advisory committee was composed of respected senior faculty, and their endorsement of the program was helpful in encouraging the participation of other faculty and advising staff. The purpose of the meeting with employers was for them to provide a brief overview of their companies and to explain the kinds of entry-level positions available and the selection criteria used in evaluating candidates. To elicit frank and candid responses from faculty and staff it was important that these kinds of discussions with employers did not have students present. The assumption was that without students present, faculty would feel more comfortable asking questions and employers would gain a better understanding of faculty concerns. Three employers from very different industries and who recently had interviewed on campus were invited to participate. The response to the program was very positive; forty-eight faculty and staff attended. As one English faculty member commented, "I found the meeting to be informative and useful. In fact, attending yesterday's session has already enabled me to be much more specific and helpful in speaking with a senior advisee today. I expect that the quality of advice I can offer students will be enhanced as a result of the information I learned from yesterday's program." An honors program adviser referred to the comments of the employers as informative and called them a "reality check" (McGrath, 1985, p. 26). Employers viewed participation in the program as a way to educate faculty about their company and the positions available; the faculty, in turn, could pass this information on to students and colleagues. These kinds of sessions were also encouraging to the career services staff, who were pleased to see faculty and academic staff interested in the career prospects of their students.

At Montana State University–Billings an advisory board was established to strengthen relationships with area employers. The advisory board is composed of five faculty representatives, twelve representatives of the area's major employers, campus administrators, and the student body president. Concerned about increasing student participation in campus career events, the board sought a way to involve faculty with area employers. A committee was organized to develop the "faculty employer connection" program for faculty volunteers to go off campus and visit employers. Student government leaders contacted faculty to encourage their participation. Faculty were positive about gaining insight into what employers expect of graduates, and employers appreciated the interest of faculty in learning more about their businesses (Reuss, 2001).

Students want to understand how what they are studying might translate into employment opportunities. Career services programs that link faculty and staff academic advisers with employers like the ones at the University of Minnesota and Montana State University–Billings are one way to improve the quality of academic advising and provide employers access to key personnel who influence students. As Reuss (2001) stated, "In the end, it is the students who reap the greatest benefits from the Faculty-Employer Connection."

**Recognizing Employers.** For many of the career services activities and programs to be successful depends upon the cooperation and participation of employers. Employers who have demonstrated a commitment to the institution and career services—by doing an exemplary job participating in campus recruiting and career and job fairs; serving as speakers to student groups, classes, and workshops; assisting in establishing or coordinating internships; and hosting student or faculty visits to their companies— deserve to be recognized. Career services staff and students can be involved in nominating and selecting the recipient(s). The criteria for recognition might include employer's cooperation in working with staff to schedule campus interview schedules, receptions, or other recruiting events; the results of student evaluations after interviewing with the recruiters, which, of course, must be confidential; and the employer's willingness to participate in campus career programs and follow through on those commitments. The recognition might be as simple as hosting a luncheon at the end of the academic year and presenting a plaque to the employer who has done an outstanding job. The persons being recognized may want to invite their supervisor to the luncheon, and the career services staff might invite senior campus administrators, faculty, and student leaders. Taking the time to recognize those employers who have done an exemplary job is well worth the effort. Campus administrators, faculty, and student leaders learn more about how the career services area works with employers, and the employers being recognized appreciates being acknowledged for doing a good job.

## Conclusion

Career services have undergone a remarkable transformation over the last thirty years from offices with limited functions and little visibility on campus to undertakings offering a broad array of valuable career assistance to students. A dramatic increase in the number of college graduates in the early 1970s and a more competitive job market challenged the utility of a college degree, particularly a liberal arts degree. Later in the decade, as competition increased for new students and colleges became more interested in attracting and retaining a more diverse student body, students expressed the need for earlier and more comprehensive career assistance. Interest in the employment prospects and salaries of college graduates continued throughout the 1980s and 1990s as the job market continued to change, tuition rose, and students accumulated greater loan debt. As career services became more visible on college campuses, they also have had to reconcile the expectations of students, senior campus administrators, development officers, faculty, and employers.

Providing students assistance in identifying and clarifying their career goals based on their interests, values, and abilities along with teaching them how to conduct a job search is the very foundation of career services. Access to employers does little good if students are not clear about their career interests and not prepared to initiate contact with employers. Career services also provides a valuable institutional function as the primary link to employers. Through interaction with employers, career services staff enhance their knowledge of the work world and become more effective and credible when advising students. While on-campus recruiting is a very popular way for students to access employers, it is neither the most effective nor the most realistic way to find employment for the majority of graduates. Many colleges and universities will not be able to attract employers on campus given their liberal arts curriculum, small enrollment, and rural location. However, other ways are available to the career services staff to facilitate employer interaction with students, faculty, and staff. Providing opportunities for faculty and academic advising staff to meet with employers enhances the quality of academic and career planning. Opportunities to interact with employers through information interviewing, shadowing, and mentoring programs help students clarify their career interests. Through cooperative education and internship programs, students experience the connection between classroom learning and work in their career field and enhance their prospects for employment after graduation. Whether a campus is small or large, career fairs can be designed to explore occupational interests with professionals, and job fairs provide opportunities for students to meet potential employers. Regardless of institutional size, location, or mission, creative career services offices with appropriate staff, operating budget, and campus office facilities can find ways to cultivate employers to help students and strengthen institutional relationships.

## References

Barbeau, J. E. *Second to None: Seventy-Five Years of Leadership in the Cooperative Education Movement.* Boston: Northeastern University, 1985.

*Gator Launch: A Minority Career Mentoring Program.* Career Resource Center, University of Florida, 2001.

Goodman, A. P., Rayman, J. R., and Ferrell, D. "The Commercialization of Career Services: Ethical Considerations for Practitioners." *Journal of Career Planning and Placement,* 2001, *61*(2), 21–27.

Hecker, D. E. "The Jam at the Bottom of the Funnel: The Outlook for College Graduates." *Occupational Outlook Quarterly,* Spring 1978, 22(1).

McGrath, G. L. "The Evolving Nature of Career Development in the Liberal Arts College." In D. H. Montross and C. J. Shinkman (eds.), *Career Development in the 1980s: Theory and Practice.* Springfield, Ill.: Thomas, 1981.

McGrath, G. L. "Strengthening 'The Weakest Link' Between Students and Employers." *Journal of College Placement,* 1985a, *45*(4), 25–27.

McGrath, G. L. "The Career Development Value of Internships." *Focus on Teaching and Learning.* Office of Development Programs, University of Minnesota, 1985b.

NACE. *Principles for Professional Conduct,* 1998.

Nagle, R., and Bohovich, J. "Career Services in the Year 2000." *Journal of Career Planning and Employment,* 2000, *60*(4), 41–47.

Reuss, P. B. "Students Reap Benefits from Faculty-Employer Connection." *Journal of Career Planning and Employment,* 2001, *61*(3), 37–39.

Rose, J. R. "Some Plain Talk on Retention by a College Dean." In L. Noel (ed.), *Reducing the Dropout Rate.* New Directions for Student Services, no. 3. San Francisco: Jossey-Bass, 1978.

Shapero, A. *Managing Professional People.* New York: Free Press, 1985.

Stewart, R. A. "Placement Services." In J. Rayman (ed.), *The Changing Role of Career Services.* New Directions for Student Services, no. 62. San Francisco: Jossey-Bass, 1993.

GARY L. MCGRATH *is dean of student affairs at Arizona State University East.*

*In recent years student affairs professionals have had
well-documented success in organizing valuable learning
experiences in the community for college students. An in-
depth review of a community-based student leadership
program at Northern Michigan University provides a
model that benefits students and the surrounding
community.*

# The Community as a Classroom

*David L. Bonsall, Rachel A. Harris, and Jill N. Marczak*

For many years student affairs professionals were challenged to make the
case that student learning included a number of extracurricular and cocurricular experiences on college campuses. Today it is widely accepted that
a student's education extends well beyond the classroom. In more recent
times student affairs staff have moved the boundaries even further to
include the communities that surround college campuses, and many have
established volunteer centers and student volunteer programs. A number of
schools have initiated structured service learning programs, often under the
leadership of student affairs professionals. Research conducted by Astin and
Sax (1998) verifies that student participants in community service and service learning experiences are learning lessons and acquiring skills that com-
plement classroom learning, introduce civic responsibility, provide
leadership experiences, and have long-term benefits. Communities, in turn,
have benefited significantly from the time and talent expended by students.
As a result, community members have demonstrated a willingness and an
enthusiasm for interacting with students. In this chapter we describe the
advantages of engaging students in their neighboring communities for
positive change, and we examine a number of successful program examples, including Northern Michigan University's Student Leadership Fellows Program.

Current times have brought into sharp focus a number of serious societal problems that have defied simple, easy solutions. The magnitude of challenges such as poverty, substance abuse, inadequate education, prejudice, lack
of support for young people, the decreasing number of role models for the
youth of our country, and the number of people who are not integrated into
our society is overwhelming. Society expects colleges and universities to play

a role in developing citizen leaders equipped to deal with these issues. For some colleges and universities, community-based leadership development programs are the answer.

## The Development of Citizen Leaders

Henry Cisneros, former Secretary for Housing and Urban Development, has said that "institutions of higher learning . . . bring formidable intellectual and economic resources to their communities. It is encouraging to report that many institutions are . . . tearing down the wall that separates campus from community, and devoting intellectual and other resources to community building. . . . [Colleges and universities] are deciding that they prefer to live together with their community rather than live apart from it" (Jacoby and others, 1996, p. 92). Without question, communities have benefited from the time, talent, energy, and enthusiasm that students have brought to bear in their respective communities through volunteer and service learning initiatives. At the same time student experiences in the community can be meaningful, enriching, and life changing.

Astin and Sax (1998) summarized their study on the effects of participating in service during the undergraduate years as "substantially enhancing the students' academic development, life skill development, and sense of civic responsibility" (p. 251). Astin, Vogelgesang, Ikeda, and Yee (2000) reported that service participation shows significant positive effects on important outcome measures: academic performance, values, self-efficacy, leadership, choice of a service career, and plans to participate in service after college (p. 4). They went on to note that these findings directly replicate other recent studies using different samples and methodologies.

Conclusions from these studies point to the ability of students to develop leadership skills and a heightened commitment to civic responsibility through service activities. Both capabilities are in high demand in society today, and provide an exciting new direction for student affairs and community partnerships in the development of citizen leaders.

## Leadership and Civic Responsibility

Today society faces formidable problems and challenges at the same time that citizen interest in addressing them is declining. Schwartz (2001) cites a 1998 report by the National Commission on Civic Renewal, "A Nation of Spectators: How Civic Disengagement Weakens America," to illustrate the need for citizen leaders. The report reveals five areas of civic concern: political participation at the national and local levels, trust in public institutions and in one another as citizens, participation in voluntary associations, personal and community security, and family integrity and strength. Astin and Astin (2000) echo similar concerns. They state that "there is mounting evidence that the quality of leadership in this country has been eroding in recent years. The list of problems is long: shaky race relations, growing economic disproportions and inequities, excessive materialism, decaying inner cities, a deteriorating infrastructure, a weakening public school system, an irresponsible mass media, declining civic engagement, and the increasing ineffectiveness of government, to name just a few" (p. 2). They go on to report that "a major problem with contemporary civic life in America is that too few of our citizens are actually engaged in efforts to effect positive social change. Viewed in this context, an important 'leadership development' challenge for higher education is to *empower* students, by helping them develop those special talents and attitudes that will enable them to become effective social change agents" (p. 2).

With growing social needs comes the expectation that colleges and universities will play a pivotal role in developing socially responsible citizen leaders. Service programs and service learning initiatives have opened the door to a community classroom where meaningful learning can occur for college students. It is reasonable to assume that as student affairs professionals seek to specifically develop citizen leaders, the community is where some of the most meaningful servant leadership and community-based leadership lessons might be learned.

## Promising Programs

Four successful community-campus leadership programs and initiatives are described here.

**The Excellence in Leadership Program.** Housed at Ball State University in Muncie, Indiana, this is a four-phase, four-year program that develops citizen leaders using three leadership theories: situational, ethical or principle-centered, and servant leadership. Phase one focuses on confidence and self-esteem; phase two focuses on involvement and student organizations; phase three focuses on servant leadership and volunteerism on campus and in the larger community; and phase four connects students with their future professions and leadership outside the university. Participants may elect to participate in the program for credit (one credit per semester for a total of eight possible credits).

Service projects occur throughout the program, with students deciding which group projects to pursue. Past projects have included Habitat for Humanity, after-school programs, nursing home activities, the Muncie Boys & Girls Club, and the Humane Society. As students progress through the program they feel good about making a difference, have an increased level of self-confidence, and are committed to civic involvement for life. Anecdotal evidence suggests continued and increased levels of volunteerism by juniors and seniors.

**Wackerle Four-Year Intentional Program.** Monmouth College in Monmouth, Illinois, recently revised its mission statement to include the goal of preparing students "for leadership, citizenship, and service in a global context." At the present time, 436 of the 1,100 enrolled students at Monmouth College participate in the Wackerle Four-Year Intentional Program that combines career preparation with leadership development and an appreciation for community service.

A significant experience for an "emerging leader" occurs in the student's second year when a senior student, called a leadership fellow, mentors him or her. As a pair, they are expected to organize and implement a hands-on community development project. As part of the process, these students reflect on the service and leadership development aspects of their project. They also consider how civic engagement will be important in their careers.

**The Leadership for Change Program.** Portland State University begins with a sophomore gateway leadership course, which leads to cluster courses in areas that include philosophy, spirituality, and law and ethics. The motto for Portland State University is "Let Knowledge Serve the City." Its Leadership for Change Program is designed according to the social change model (Higher Education Research Institute, 1996). Through a "Leadership for Change" class, students reflect upon and connect their values to real-life experiences, take their learning to a deeper level, and expand their definitions of leadership. The opportunity to learn from the community is "an amazing opportunity for students" according to the campus assistant director of student development.

**Leadership Development Experience and Mentor Program.** A segment of the LeaderQuest Series at the University of Minnesota is notable because it was one of the early leadership development initiatives to match student participants with a community mentor. Mentors, all of whom are thirty-five or older, are recruited from both on and off campus, from business, industry, education, and other fields. Mentors are trained at the start of the program, and four occasions are set aside during the semester where mentors and students socialize at an organized event.

LeaderQuest staff send a monthly newsletter to students and mentors with ideas on what to talk about, how to close the relationship, and other useful information regarding mentoring. Program staff members are always available to provide support to the mentors and mentees during the process.

## The Student Leader Fellowship Program at Northern Michigan University

The Student Leader Fellowship Program (SLFP) at Northern Michigan University in Marquette is an innovative leadership program dedicated to developing competent, ethical, and community-centered student leaders. SLFP was initiated in 1991 under the combined sponsorship of the W. K. Kellogg Foundation and Northern Michigan University. Two distinguishing characteristics of the SLFP are its focus on community-based leadership and reliance on community assets.

SLFP is an intensive two-year experience. Fifty new students are selected each year, which translates into approximately one hundred participants engaged with the program at one time. Selection criteria include leadership potential and the ability to make a two-year commitment.

During their two-year experience, student fellows complete a total of six program components. Each component provides participants with a variety of structured experiences to strengthen and enhance their leadership skills and to help build a lifelong commitment to service at the community level. Moreover, program components address one or more of the three SLFP goals, which are:

- To provide student fellows with a conceptual framework in which to assess, develop, and strengthen leadership abilities.
- To create opportunities for student fellows to practice and experience leadership roles and to gain confidence in their leadership abilities.
- To create an awareness and understanding by student fellows of community-based problems, processes, and grass-roots problem solving, and to instill a commitment towards community-based leadership.

Program components are described below with particular attention given to the mentoring and the community service internship facets because of the inclusion of community resources.

**Fall Retreat.** Each fall an overnight fall retreat is conducted at an off-campus location for the one hundred program participants. Retreat goals are to help new student fellows learn more about the program, acquaint student fellows with one another and with program staff, and to build a strong commitment to SLFP.

**Leadership Theory and Practice Course.** This is a two-credit course that introduces new student fellows to leadership theories and concepts. At the conclusion of the course, student fellows complete a self-assessment or action plan for their own leadership development. "How to make a difference" at the local level and "servant leadership" are themes of the class, with a class highlight being a session where community leaders discuss problem-solving strategies in the local area.

**Skill Builder! Workshops.** Each semester approximately twenty-five Skill Builder! workshops are presented. Topics include such things as "Caring for Group Members," "Archie Bunker's Neighborhood—A Diversity Exercise," "Tips on Public Speaking," and "Stress—Use It Or Lose It." Fellows are required to participate in fifteen workshops over the course of their two-year program. Members of the local community are frequently Skill Builder! presenters.

**Special Occasions.** "Special Occasions" are opportunities for student fellows to meet notable leaders and special guests who are visiting either the university or the Marquette community to hear their thoughts on leadership, ask questions, and spend informal time with them. Local leaders are also featured. SLFP sponsors the "Leader in Residence" program, which annually hosts a prominent leader on campus for a couple of days of classroom visits, presentations, and student group meetings. Community mentors and community service internship site advisers are invited and encouraged to attend these events.

**Mentors.**  Each of the fifty new student fellows is assigned a mentor for his or her first year in the program. Mentors are community leaders (defined as anyone who is making a difference in the local area) who act as role models, advisers, and teachers. A primary goal of the mentor component is for fellows to become better acquainted with community problems, opportunities, organizational and governmental processes, and leadership possibilities.

Mentor recruitment is ongoing, but most mentors are recruited during the summer. Over the decade, 364 members of the local community have served as mentors; many have done so on multiple occasions. Mentors attend an orientation in August, where the goals and expectations of the mentoring component are discussed and an overview of SLFP is shared. At their orientation mentors are given the name of their student fellow and some information about the individual.

Mentoring matches are based on information provided on an individual profile that student fellows complete in March and mentors submit during the summer. The goal is to match students and mentors who share common interests.

Student fellows and their mentors attend a Mentorshop in September where expectations, goals, and concerns are shared and each pair has an opportunity to plan activities. The mentoring relationship is further solidified with a Mentor Biography assignment during the early weeks of the leadership class and with a second Mentorshop in January. Over the course of the year each pair is expected to get together on a biweekly basis. Activities include lunches, community organization meetings, conferences, workshops, hobbies, and attendance at community and campus events.

Anne Zanotti, recent graduate of SLFP, wrote in her reflection paper at the conclusion of her term, "Having a mentor has been the most influential experience for me. My mentor is such a wonderful role model for me and I feel so lucky that she was my mentor. I was nervous at first to meet her, but we got along so well. She took me in as if I were one of her own. She has been a great asset in my college life, and I couldn't have asked for a better mentor."

For eleven years mentors have been instrumental in modeling community-based leadership for program participants. They share their experiences, discuss their perceptions on leadership, offer advice, and provide students with feedback that aids in their leadership development. The influence of mentors often goes well beyond the one-year relationship that the program calls for. Significant numbers of fellows have remained in contact with their mentors for years. In his reflection paper on the SLFP experience, student Jason Coleman wrote, "The most influential component of the SLFP (for me) was the mentoring component. My mentor has and still does provide me with the guidance and advice that has helped me make my SLFP experience memorable."

Mentors have been instrumental in the growth and development of SLFP. Many recruit additional members of the community to serve as mentors, others help present Skill Builder! Workshops, and some contribute financially to the program and assist in the creation of new community services internship sites. Mentors have become true stakeholders in the development of these students as community leaders of the future.

**Community Service Internships.** During the second year of SLFP student fellows put their leadership skills into action and gain an appreciation for service and leadership at the local level through a Community Service Internship (CSI). These internships provide student participants with an opportunity to be part of the leadership of a community project. Fellows design their internships, choosing from existing sites or a variety of new possibilities. Some elect to do their CSI with a team of other student fellows while others prefer to engage in the community on an individual basis. Each site is required, however, to have a CSI adviser who is a member of the community working at, or involved with, the chosen internship site. Program staff assist students as they develop their community service internship sites to ensure that SLFP criteria are met: a challenging yet realistic mission, an opportunity to provide leadership, an appropriate time commitment, and a project that is truly volunteer in nature. In consultation with the site adviser, interns develop goals for the experience, which are approved by the SLFP staff. Internships involve a commitment of from four to six hours a week.

An SLFP staff member meets with each new CSI adviser before an internship begins. The term of the internship normally spans the academic year, although individual circumstances sometimes require other arrangements. Student fellows meet as needed with their site adviser and also meet once a month as a group with SLFP staff to share experiences, maintain a sense of fellowship, and build coalitions between projects where feasible. Before completing the CSI each student writes a reflection paper that describes the project, how the goals were met, and lessons learned from the experience.

Since 1992 student fellows at Northern Michigan University have been involved in 145 different community internship sites at which they have volunteered in excess of forty-two thousand hours of their time. Examples of CSI experiences include advising the Lake Superior Village (low-income housing project) Youth Council, volunteering at Harbor House (domestic violence shelter), assisting with various programs at the Upper Peninsula Children's Museum, coaching youth sports teams, conducting art projects at elementary schools, working with Home Hospice, volunteering as a mentor for youth referred through the court system, coordinating projects at the Moosewood Nature Center, and advising a middle-school newspaper staff.

The effect of the Community Service Internship experience on student fellows is considerable, as evidenced by the comments made in reflection papers. Student Jon Barch developed an internship at a new site, the North Star Academy, an alternative high school, where he and his teacher-supervisor planned, organized, and implemented a leadership development program for the students. He reflected that "the experiences I have had through my internship have affected me tremendously as an individual. I have gained much knowledge, increased my leadership skills, boosted my confidence, made invaluable connections in this community, and learned a lot about my abilities as well as the limits of those abilities. In the co-teaching portion of my duties, I was constantly engaged in discussing the theoretical aspect of leadership."

Although student fellows grow as leaders as a result of their Community Service Internships, the Marquette community also benefits. As site adviser Cheryl Lorge of the Women's Center and Harbor House stated, "The student fellows are one of our biggest assets. It has been a pleasure working with them. They become an extension of our staff. I have found the students to be dependable, honest, kind, caring, compassionate, and seeking to truly making a difference. They have great interactions with the women and children. We find they learn so much and keep coming back for a second or third year."

Another site adviser, Karen Anderson at the local Gwinn Area Community School, says, "The Student Leader Fellowship Program is mutually beneficial. Students have the opportunity to be creative and demonstrate their initiative and leadership skills, while completing a service project that is practical and useful to the community."

Will Keim, the university's intercollegiate chaplain, states, "The Student Leader Fellowship Program at Northern Michigan University is a shining example of town and gown cooperation and collaboration. Students are placed in real life situations that enhance the in-classroom learning. A series of sequential experiences results in a student ready to enter the work force and a community that realizes the benefit and potential of the university in their own backyard. It is an amazing blend of curricular and co-curricular learning wonderfully consistent with the characteristics of the millennial students."

## Impact of Northern Michigan University's Student Leader Fellowship Program

SLFP has drawn successfully on community resources to teach students about leadership at the local level and, in the process, has developed citizen leaders who, it is hoped, will be engaged citizens for years to come. Since 1995 student participants have taken a pre- and a postindividual assessment survey. One question asks students to assess the extent of their future commitment to volunteering in "this or another community." Before they start their SLFP experience, the average number of student fellows who answer "to a great extent" is 43 percent. Upon completion of the program, this number has risen to an average of 80 percent. Program graduates respond yearly to a requested update on their careers, families, and civic engagements among other things. This information is then shared in an alumni newsletter. Alumni repeatedly report their continuing involvement in community service activities postgraduation.

SLFP has been a positive venture for Northern Michigan University as well. Its president, Dr. Judith Bailey, concludes, "The Student Leader Fellowship Program is a point of pride at NMU. Students are attracted to Northern because of the opportunity to be actively engaged in leadership and service learning. Once involved, the SLFP students become campus and community leaders—using the change in their own lives to help change others. Character development is essential in a world where students' values and beliefs are challenged daily. The graduates of the SLFP are grounded with both a sense of self, commitment to their personal values, and a vision of how they can individually make a difference in the community."

Anecdotal information attests to how the city of Marquette has benefited from their investment in SLFP. City commissioner and former Marquette mayor, Cameron Howes, comments, "Students are assigned to a number of different organizations within the local community to hone their leadership skills. In addition to the growth that the students experience, our local organizations benefit enormously through the time, enthusiasm, energy, and creativity that the fellows bring. A very important side effect of the program has been that it has brought the community much closer to the university, resulting in many other cooperative ventures." Members of the Marquette community continue to volunteer in large numbers as mentors, internship site advisers, and workshop presenters. Their ongoing support is another indicator of the program's success.

## Lessons Learned

The development of a leadership program in cooperation with the surrounding community provides for a unique set of challenges and opportunities. Staff members at NMU have learned valuable lessons for application at other campuses.

- *Identify dedicated staff positions.* Leadership development programs in general require staff that will make the program a priority. A few hours of attention each week will not suffice. This is especially true when developing a leadership program around community involvement. It takes considerable time and effort to build and maintain successful relationships, to train community volunteers, and to communicate regularly with all the parties.

- *Institutionalize the leadership program.* Community-based leadership development programs, when done properly, result in positive benefits for schools and their host communities. A long-term commitment by university resources saves time and effort that can be devoted to the core program. Support and encouragement from university officials ensures more program visibility and appeal in the community.
- *Build relationships in the community.* Long-term and widespread community support for a leadership program requires extensive citizen involvement. This requires time and effort by staff. Activities such as recruiting and training mentors, arranging for volunteer projects, and coordinating internship sites are never-ending.
- *Select responsible participants.* As with any leadership program, participant selection is critical. Participants become university ambassadors to the external community. Moreover, responsible students also will ensure the continued interest of community volunteers and a pipeline of new recruits.
- *Tailor the program to school and community realities.* Just as no two colleges have the same characteristics, communities are also different. When building a community-based program, it is essential to base it upon the realities not only of the institution and its student body but also on the characteristics of the surrounding communities.
- *Take time to develop community-based leadership programs.* Strong community relationships, connections, and program awareness do not occur overnight. It is a gradual process that occurs over a period of years through sustained effort. Again, the host institution must commit to the community for an extended period of time.
- *Share ownership of the program.* Token community involvement in a community-based program will not work. Although university program staff provide program continuity, other parties must feel that there is sufficient flexibility, trust, and joint ownership to maintain their involvement.
- *Use flexible scheduling.* Students and community mentors and volunteers are busy people. When scheduling events like Northern Michigan University's Mentorshops or mentor-orientation sessions, it is necessary to schedule multiple sessions so that participants may choose a convenient time that fits their schedules. These people have families and careers, and time is their most precious resource.
- *Ensure that community involvement is structured.* Citizens are willing to do considerably more than asked if the cause is a good one and expectations are clearly defined. Individuals often are hesitant to become involved with open-ended commitments, but are willing to participate when duties are laid out and the program structure is evident.
- *Implement training programs for citizen volunteers.* The college campus is unfamiliar territory for many citizens in the surrounding community. A significant number of community volunteers for a leadership development program might be somewhat intimidated by the prospect because of uncertainty regarding the experiences and skills required to be helpful

to a college student. When volunteers are well-oriented and reassured as to what they have to offer, most find the experience to be highly rewarding—and a learning experience for themselves as well.

## Conclusion

The communities that surround colleges and universities have the potential to provide students with significant learning experiences. A campus community program takes time to cultivate and requires vision, resources, effective communication, and openness to doing things in a different way. Campus community programs need to be tailored to the unique characteristics of each university, student body, and community. Although the investment is substantial, the return can be great. Students are able to learn from real-life settings in surroundings that will be their future homes. Universities and communities are able to work together on a positive mutually beneficial project that helps build a bridge for future collaborations. The investment in a campus community leadership project for students, if carefully planned and considered, is a fruitful venture for a university or college.

## References

Astin, A. W., and Astin, H. S. *Leadership Reconsidered: Engaging Higher Education in Social Change*. Battle Creek, Mich.: W.K. Kellogg Foundation, January 2000.

Astin, A. W., and Sax, L. J. "How Undergraduates Are Affected by Service Participation." *Journal of College Student Development*, 1998, 39(3), 251–263.

Astin, A. W., Vogelgesang, L. J., Ikeda, E. K., and Yee, J. A. *How Service Learning Affects Students*. Los Angeles: Higher Education Research Institute, University of California–Los Angeles, Jan. 2000.

Higher Education Research Institute. *A Social Change Model of Leadership Development*. Los Angeles: Higher Education Research Institute, University of California–Los Angeles, Jan. 1996.

Jacoby, B., and Associates. *Service-Learning in Higher Education*. San Francisco: Jossey-Bass, 1996.

Schwartz, S. W. "Leadership for What?" *About Campus*, 2001, 6(2), 13–17.

DAVID L. BONSALL *is director of student activities and leadership programs at Northern Michigan University and is the cocoordinator of the Student Leader Fellowship Program.*

RACHEL A. HARRIS *is the assistant director of student activities and leadership programs at Northern Michigan University and is the cocoordinator of the Student Leader Fellowship Program.*

JILL N. MARCZAK *is a graduate assistant in the Student Activities and Leadership Programs Office at Northern Michigan University.*

8

*This chapter discusses the role of external partnerships in student development and learning outcomes assessment in the context of results from a national survey of senior student affairs officers.*

# External Partners in Assessment of Student Development and Learning

*Marilee J. Bresciani*

Banta, Black, and Kline (2001) address the importance of conducting outcomes assessment in student affairs by stating that "governors, legislators, and accrediting bodies made it clear that higher education, like every other service in which the public invests, needs to provide credible evidence of the value and effectiveness of its programs. More importantly, assessment is a means of discovering new information about our programs that will help us improve them" (p. 1). Constituents' escalating demands for performance accountability, accreditation requirements, and a desire to meet principles such as those created by the Council for the Advancement of Standards call for senior student affairs officers to provide evidence that their programs are accomplishing what they desire them to be accomplishing. In this chapter we articulate the importance of assessment, outline the barriers to assessment, and discuss the role of external partnerships in student development and learning outcomes assessment in the context of results from a national survey of senior student affairs officers.

As Upcraft and Schuh (1996) illustrated, senior student affairs officers have been challenged to provide justification for the cost of the services

The author is grateful for the assistance of two gifted research assistants, Caryn Sabourin and Katja Remlinger. Remlinger assisted with data analysis. Sabourin, along with Dr. Jo Allen, vice provost for undergraduate affairs at North Carolina State University, and Dr. Dean Bresciani, associate vice chancellor for student services at the University of North Carolina–Chapel Hill, assisted in the design of the survey. Chris Rogus, a North Carolina State computer science undergraduate, was key in making this survey Web-enabled. Thank you to all of you!

they provide. A now inarguable trend seems to be that as resources continue to tighten, student affairs professionals will be required to provide direct and indirect evidence that their programs are having an effect on student learning and development. In addition, increased emphasis on undergraduate program review and institutional effectiveness require all those participating in the success of students to report their accomplishments. Through assessment, student affairs practitioners will be considerably better positioned to improve their programs and provide proof of their accomplishments when resource allocations and other forms of support are in question.

If done in a meaningful manner, assessment in student affairs could reinforce or emphasize the mission of each student affairs unit; modify, shape, and improve programs and/or performance (for example, *formative,* meaning "to form or shape the program or performance"); critique a program's quality or value compared to the program's previously defined principles (for example, *summative,* meaning "to make judgments about the result"); inform planning; inform decision making; inform the request for additional funds from the university and external community; and assist in meeting accreditation requirements, models of best practices, and national benchmarks.

## What Are the Steps Involved in Assessing Outcomes?

In agreement with Upcraft and Schuh (1996), Anderson (2001) wrote that one of the reasons many higher education professionals are not successful in implementing meaningful continuous assessment is that they do not approach it in a systematic way. Whether writing assessment plans or reporting assessment results for the purposes of accountability or for continuous improvement, an outline can aid organization and ensure inclusion of the most important assessment elements.

The following is an assessment plan outline based on the writings and work of Palomba and Banta (1999), Gordon and Habley (2000), Helm (2001), Upcraft and Schuh (1996), the Southern Association of Colleges and Schools (2001), and the North Carolina State University Committee on Undergraduate Academic Program Review (2001).

   I. *Unit or program mission:* State the unit or program mission.
  II. *Unit or program goals or objectives:* Generally describe what the unit intends to accomplish and illustrate the purposes for assessment.
 III. *Learning and development outcomes:* Specifically describe what the program must do; express what students, faculty, and staff must know and do. These learning outcomes must be measurable and meaningful. It is not necessary to have an outcome for every aspect of the program. It may be helpful to divide the outcomes into categories, as applicable, such as (1) intended program outcomes, (2) student learning

outcomes, (3) student development outcomes, (4) faculty development outcomes, and (5) staff development outcomes.

IV. *Evaluation methods:* Indicate how the learning outcomes have been met. Specify what you are looking for and how you will find it. It may be helpful to organize this section by the outcomes.

V. *Implementation of assessment:* Describe who will be doing what and when they will be doing it. The time-line should demonstrate the commitment to continuous assessment.

VI. *Results:* What did the results of the assessment show? What was learned about the objectives you stated in section III? What was the assessment plan not able to tell you?

VII. *Decisions and recommendations:* Based on the results, what decisions were made about program, planning, policy, budgeting, and the assessment plan? What was changed? What was kept?

## If Outcomes Assessment Is That Simple, Why Don't More People Use It?

Academic and student affairs units engaged in continuous assessment can testify to its many meaningful applications. Although the many benefits of assessment seem clear, Brown (2001) has illustrated several reasons that faculty may not want to participate in assessment. Student affairs professionals, as well as other administrators, may share these reasons.

Brown states that many do not join in assessment for one or more of the following reasons. Faculty and administrators may be convinced that assessment is just another fad and may not want to take time away from their already overcommitted schedules to check out the latest rage. Also, they may have no more time to give to yet another project; wonder what the direct, personal benefits are for them; believe that they are already conducting assessment and wonder why others don't recognize that; fear that the results of their assessment could be used against them in their tenure process, merit review, annual program review, personnel review, or to harm their reputations; or think they are doing just fine and thus do not need a formal process to prove it.

Additional reasons for resisting engagement in assessment could include that faculty and administrators do not have access to the resources to help them conduct assessment (research assistants, analysis tools, assessment administration, and analysis support); may be overwhelmed by the results, may not know what to do with the results, or may be unsure of how to communicate the meaning of the data; may fear that the data will be reported irresponsibly causing rash and careless decisions to be made; may resist changing-improving programs that the assessment results show need changing (similar to that posed by Fultz and Wong, 2001); may be concerned with the political implications or the public relations issues resulting from assessment findings; and finally, may feel that their authority or credibility will be compromised because they are unfamiliar with assessment terminology, standards, processes, and instruments. The fear of saying the wrong thing can be stifling and can cause assessment conversations to falter before they even begin.

Other barriers to participation in assessment can come from the assessment professionals themselves. Some may fear that by clearly and concisely defining assessment to faculty and administrators, the assessment professional's expertise and terminology will be trivialized by people not recognizing its complexities. They may also feel that a little knowledge is a dangerous thing and that the nonexperts empowered to participate in the assessment process may actually end in making a bigger mess of things. They may also fear that if others begin doing assessment, they could lose their value and academic credibility among their colleagues as well as lose their jobs.

Brown (2001) addresses solutions to these concerns. She emphasizes that acknowledging that these reasons exist and communicating that understanding and concern to faculty and administrators may alleviate some of the anxiety surrounding assessment. She further points out that institutions can move assessment forward by providing resources, professional development, institutional support, rewards, and evidence that the organization is committed to assessment. Banta, Black, and Kline (2001) encourage administrators to celebrate and share their assessment successes while Fultz and Wong (2001) emphasize the importance of understanding the faculty culture and lifestyle first before even introducing assessment.

These are very helpful solutions indeed. This author extends them by recommending that we also equip faculty, student affairs administrators, and staff with the language to enter into the assessment conversation. Although this approach might pose the danger of excluding an assessment professional's preferred definition, it may also provide the catalyst that is needed for those who are standing on the sidelines to enter into the conversation, to feel safe about asking questions, to feel the support they desire to succeed or fail in their assessment efforts, and to feel empowered to move forward in their assessment efforts.

Finally, engagement in collaborative partnerships can provide tools to overcome many barriers to assessment. Banta, Black, and Kline (2001) write, "Good assessment is based fundamentally on collaboration among colleagues" (p. 1). External collaborations may be beneficial as well.

## So, Where Can I Go for Help?

One solution to moving toward continuous and systematic assessment is to engage in partnerships with external constituents. Many excellent partnerships and tools are available to student affairs professionals. Several are outlined in Upcraft and Schuh (1996) and in Borden and Zak Owens (2001). Other lists of tools may be found on the Web, such as the American College

Personnel Association (ACPA)'s "Commission IX Assessment for Student Development" (1999).

In order to gain a better understanding of how senior student affairs officers are utilizing external partners in assessment, North Carolina State University in partnership with the National Association for Student Personnel Administrators (NASPA) administered an on-line survey in the summer of 2001 to determine how senior student affairs officers (SSAOs) conducted and used outcomes assessment. In particular, this author sought to understand if and why an SSAO turns to external national organizations, either for profit or not for profit, to assess outcomes in student affairs.

Three hundred and ninety-eight senior student affairs officers were randomly selected to participate in this study. Participants were senior student affairs officers who are members of NASPA and have an e-mail address on file with NASPA. Participation was completely voluntary and confidential. Twenty-two SSAOs never received the e-mail invitation to participate in the survey, and three were unable to access the on-line survey. One hundred and fifty-two SSAOs or their designees completed the survey resulting in a response rate of 40.8 percent. Several Carnegie classifications (method of classifying institutions) were represented in the respondents. The categories of largest percentage of representation to least were Masters II with 20.8 percent, Masters I with 14.2 percent, Baccalaureate Liberal Arts with 13.3 percent, Associates Arts and Doctoral Extensive with 10.0 percent each, and Doctoral Intensive with 9.2 percent. In response to the majority of the survey questions, respondents could check all that apply; thus, most response percentages did not total one hundred.

Of those who responded, 85 percent conduct student affairs outcomes assessment and 15 percent do not. Of the 15 percent who do not perform student affairs outcomes assessment, the number-one reason for not doing so was insufficient staff time. Second was limited resources. Third was limited staff expertise in conducting assessment.

When stepwise and forward regressions were run in an attempt to predict why institutions do not conduct outcomes assessment, the variables of "limited time", "limited expertise", "limited resources", and an attitudinal variable that "the benefits of assessment are not substantial enough" emerged consistently with an $R^2$ of .81.

Would student affairs professionals feel differently if they turned to external groups for assessment help? Entities such as the Higher Education Research Institute, National Survey of Student Engagement, Noel-Levitz, American College Testing Postsecondary Services (ACT), Educational Testing Service, and College Board, to name a few, can provide senior student affairs officers with a wide selection of standardized outcomes surveys. These partners are also willing to enter into agreements to sample the student population, administer surveys, analyze the results, provide peer comparisons, and interpret results. This indeed would appear to resolve the survey-identified barriers of lack of time and expertise. However, what about the concern of limited resources?

If limited resources mean inadequate funds to purchase instruments and analyze data, then perhaps another solution is needed. That solution might lie in reallocating resources toward assessment or looking to others for assistance. As Schuh and Upcraft (2001) state, "If these costs are the only reason that assessment cannot be done, we advise the department head to go get some help—from the vice president, from another department, from a grant, or some other source on or off campus. No assessment project conducted by campus staff is so expensive that the cost of supplies should stop the project" (p. 4).

Of those SSAOs who reported conducting student affairs outcomes assessment, 92 percent did so to make decisions for program improvement, 76 percent to satisfy accreditation bodies, and 63 percent to inform funding requests and budget decisions. Forward and stepwise regression equations were run to predict why an institution conducts assessment. The variables that entered into the regression equation with an $R^2$ of .65 were "making decisions for program improvement" and "satisfying accreditation bodies." Upcraft and Schuh (1996) as well as Palomba and Banta (1999) have stated that these indeed are reasons for motivating professionals to engage in assessment.

How do SSAOs conduct assessment? Of the senior student affairs officers, 95 percent indicated that they used surveys to conduct outcomes assessment; 67 percent reported using focus groups, while 45 percent indicated that they employed peer comparisons and benchmarks to conduct outcomes assessment. As previously mentioned, many external firms and agencies are known to provide outcomes assessment survey instruments and some can even provide peer comparisons or national benchmarks for that survey data. Consultants and internal professionals can offer assistance in designing quality focus groups and interviews while national organizations such as the American Association for Higher Education can provide samples of tools to measure dimensions (e.g., rubrics), assuming a program is aware of its intended outcomes.

So how many institutions take advantage of external partners' assessment tools and services? Of the senior student affairs professionals, 82 percent use assessment tools that were developed by professional staff at their campus, followed by 61 percent who use instruments developed by external groups. Of survey participants, 75 percent who answered that their institution does conduct student affairs outcomes assessment reported that the interested professionals within student affairs administer the assessment tools, followed by 36 percent reporting that the university or college assessment officer takes on this responsibility. Finally, just 33 percent report using external partners to administer assessment instruments.

When asked who analyzes the assessment data, the same order holds true with different percentages.

| | |
|---|---|
| Interested professionals within student affairs: | 71 percent |
| University or college assessment officer: | 45 percent |
| External partners: | 43 percent |

(It is important to note the difference in percentage of SSAOs reporting who use external vendors to administer assessment tools and the percentage who use external partners for data analysis. The reader should not assume that the 33 percent who use surveys is represented in the 43 percent who contract data analysis.) The listing of who interprets the assessment data comes in a slightly different order.

| | |
|---|---|
| Interested professionals within student affairs: | 76 percent |
| University-college assessment officer: | 39 percent |
| Student affairs assessment officer: | 27 percent |
| External partners: | 24 percent |

Senior student affairs officers are employing external firms for some assessment tasks, but not to the extent they are turning to professionals within their own institution. Does this situation change based on the type of assessment that is conducted?

**Program Outcomes.** When asked what types of outcomes senior student affairs officers were assessing, 93 percent of the SSAOs, who conduct assessment, were assessing program outcomes; however no one reported using outside partners to assist in assessing program outcomes. For the purpose of this survey, program outcomes were defined as those outcomes that illustrate the results of what you want your program to accomplish. Program outcomes do not address specific student learning and development outcomes; rather they address program satisfaction, timeliness in service or product delivery, and other outcomes that would address program goals. An example of a program outcome would be that "the Women's Center will host three stress management workshops that will meet an overall student satisfaction level of 3.5 or higher on a five-point scale." Another example for an orientation program might be that "97 percent of the orientation participants will agree or strongly agree that orientation programs provided information and assistance that were helpful to their transition into the university."

Respondents reported that they are more likely to assess program outcomes in the following areas:

| | |
|---|---|
| Financial aid: | 76 percent |
| Campus security: | 74 percent |
| Honors-scholars programs: | 74 percent |
| TRIO grant programs: | 73 percent |
| First-year experience-seminars: | 70 percent |
| Living learning communities: | 61 percent |

New-student orientation (freshmen and transfers):    58 percent

Internships:    47 percent

Student housing:    45 percent

**Student Development Outcomes.** Seventy-three percent are assessing student development outcomes, and of that group, 52 percent of the SSAOs reported using external partners to aid in this type of assessment. In this survey student development outcomes were defined as outcomes that illustrate the affective domains, such as the attitudes and values one desires to instill or enhance. An example of a development outcome for a first-year program might be that "students will demonstrate an increase in their self-esteem as measured by a pre- and posttest standardized instrument." Another example for a leadership program is that "students will demonstrate responsible leadership by organizing an event that their group's membership deems important and relevant to the university community."

Respondents reported that they most often assess student development outcomes in the following areas:

Campus security:    52 percent

Honors-scholars programs:    45 percent

First-year experience-seminars:    40 percent

Financial aid:    40 percent

TRIO grant programs:    40 percent

Student organizations:    35 percent

New-student orientation (freshmen and transfers):    30 percent

**Student Learning Outcomes.** Finally, 56 percent reported that they measure student learning outcomes, in which 42 percent use external partner assistance. Student learning outcomes were defined as outcomes that exemplify learning, such as increased critical thinking and mastery of cognitive material. An example of a student learning outcome for a Living Learning Community Program might be that "students will demonstrate increased critical thinking skills in their joint first-year-experience general education inquiry courses and accompanying cocurricular experiences during their first academic year as measured by a pre- and posttest standardized instrument." Another example for student conduct is that "Student Conduct Board members will increase critical thinking skills by demonstrating a deeper level of discussion and reflection when considering student misconduct cases."

Respondents reported that they most often assess student learning outcomes in the following areas:

Student organizations:    29 percent

Campus security:    27 percent

Minority affairs:    25 percent

| | |
|---|---|
| TRIO grant programs: | 21 percent |
| Financial aid: | 19 percent |
| International student services: | 17 percent |

What explains the differences in these numbers? Is it that student affairs professionals have more expertise, or have more access to expertise with program outcomes, and thus feel more confident developing instruments that assess program outcomes and less confident developing those that assess student development and learning? Do SSAOs value program outcomes more than student learning and development outcomes and therefore measure what they value, or are they simply valuing what they can measure?

Why is it that there are fewer programs assessing student learning outcomes? Is it because of limited time to assess the latter, or is it limited expertise? Is it because SSAOs have not identified student learning outcomes in some of their areas of responsibility? Or is it because there are so few tools available for assessing student learning? Are SSAOs just unaware of the assistance that external assessment partners can provide in measuring student learning and development outcomes?

## Examples of External Partner Assistance

External partners provide viable solutions to assessing student learning and development outcomes as well as program outcomes. Before identifying some of the many partner solutions it is extremely important to note that there is no one instrument or assessment method that can provide SSAOs with all of the information they need to assess all of their program and student learning and development outcomes. In addition, each instrument has its own particular set of assets and limitations which may vary by institution and which may be apparent only after having used the tool. In some instances, the external agency will provide information about the benefits and disadvantages of its assessment tools. The purpose of this section is to introduce the SSAO to just a few of the many possible solutions.

**Program Outcomes.** Two outside providers, which offer student satisfaction surveys among other instruments and services, include the American College Testing (ACT) Postsecondary Services and Noel-Levitz. ACT offers a standardized student satisfaction survey, called the Student Opinion Survey. There is a Student Opinion Survey designed for both two-year programs and four-year programs. Using a five-point Likert scale, the survey asks students to reply to a number of satisfaction measures on topics such as academic issues, admissions, rules and policies, facilities, registration, and other general items. In addition, ACT offers specific instruments designed to measure satisfaction of academic advising and financial aid.

Interact Communications offers a protocol for student satisfaction surveys and focus groups that they will customize for any institution.

Noel-Levitz offers a student satisfaction survey that also assesses students' service priorities. This survey requests that students respond not only with their level of satisfaction for particular services but also with their perception of the importance of the service. By comparing the responses of these two factors, SSAOs may determine to some extent the correlation between students' satisfaction with a service and their perceived importance of that service.

Organizations such as ACT, Noel-Levitz, the National Survey of Student Engagement (NSSE), or the Higher Education Research Institute (HERI) will provide institutional comparisons of student satisfaction with peer schools and national norms as well. Moreover, as discussed earlier, external partners are available to help an institution choose its sample population, administer the survey, conduct analysis, and provide a summary of the results. All that is left for the institution to do is to close the assessment loop by using the results to make decisions for continuous program improvement.

**Student Development Outcomes.** Student development outcomes begin to become more elusive as one struggles to identify exactly what outcomes are educationally important and whether or not designed programs are producing those outcomes. In some circumstances SSAOs may be guilty of avoiding an assessment of student development outcomes because they are not able to articulate what they want to achieve.

If SSAOs do define student development outcomes, then they can look to several external partners to assist with their assessment. For example, the College Student Experience Questionnaire (CSEQ), the Your First College Year Survey (YFCY), and the Cooperative Institutional Research Program's survey (CIRP), along with NSSE, allow one to assess a student's level of self-reported development on a number of scales. While variances in each instrument exist, SSAOs can generally use these instruments to measure students' patterns of behavior, values, and attitudes; satisfaction with curricular and cocurricular activities; and feelings of personal success.

Other instruments such as the Rosenburg (1965) Self-Esteem Inventory (ROSE) is used to assess self-esteem in a pretest-posttest analysis. The Defining Issues Test (DIT) (Rest, 1979) or the Social Reflection Questionnaire (Gibbs and Widaman, 1992) measure moral development. The Student Adaptation to College Questionnaire (SACQ) (Baker and Siryk, 1989) is one of the many self-report surveys that measures student academic, social, personal, emotional, and general adjustment to college. The Learning and Study Strategies Inventory (LASSI) (Weinstein, Palmer, and Schulte, 1987) measures learning and study strategies using subscales such as attention, motivation, anxiety, information processing, study skills, and test-taking strategies. In the area of career development, instruments such as the Career Development Inventory College and University Form (Super and others, 1981) assist program leaders to address students' knowledge and attitudes toward career choice while evaluating career counseling programs.

**Student Learning Outcomes.**  Finally, learning outcomes appear to be even more difficult for SSAOs to assess. Again, it may be because they do not articulate any student learning outcomes for their programs. And if they do, how do they begin to provide evidence that their program has contributed to the learning they see or desire to observe? Again, external partners can provide some solutions.

The NSSE, CSEQ, and YFCY provide some indirect evidence of learning outcomes. Providing direct evidence is a bit more difficult but achievable. There are three primary assessment tools to document direct evidence of critical thinking: the Cornell Critical Thinking Test (Ennis and Millman, 1964), the California Critical Thinking Skills Test (Facione and Facione, 1998) and the Critical Thinking Appraisal (CTA) (Watson and Glaser, 1980). If you are interested in assessing critical thinking dispositions, then you could use the California Critical Thinking Disposition Inventory (Facione and Facione, 1992).

Problem Solving can be assessed using the Problem Solving Inventory (PSI) (Heppner, 1988). Other external partners in assessing intellectual development include the Measure of Epistemological Reflection (MER) (Baxter-Magdola and Porterfield, 1985) and the Measure of Intellectual Development (MID) (Knelfelkamp and Widick, 1974). Although individual scholars developed some of these instruments, many of these scholars are available for consultation on the most effective and efficient use of their tools. They also may provide analysis and interpretation assistance.

## What Is Still Needed?

The author's survey of SSAOs showed that the number-one need in the field of outcomes assessment not currently being served by external national vendors is help with assessment tool design. This is followed by assessment study design, and the provision of benchmarking and comparative data. The third most unmet need is in the interpretation of findings, followed by writing of the final report, and data collection. Can external partners in higher education help with all of these needs?

As mentioned, although some external partnerships in assessing student outcomes are taking place at the program outcomes assessment level, there remain unmet needs. Furthermore, there may be other institutional assessment needs that were not included in the author's survey, such as requiring help in

- Planning and implementing systematic assessment
- Learning how to create one's own assessment tools and methods, especially those that provide direct evidence of learning
- Making decisions and/or recommendations that need to be made based on the results

- Identifying additional information that needs to be collected because the results from the external partner(s) are inconclusive
- Bridging the gap between the common language and shared conceptual understanding of assessment and its practice
- Creating a culture where continuous improvement is the norm and outcomes assessment is expected and substantially rewarded in a meaningful manner
- Providing assistance with qualitative analysis
- Making continuous systematic assessment affordable

Can the institution alone fill some of these needs? Or should colleges and universities turn to external partners to fill the gaps?

Indeed, some SSAOs are turning to external partners and private consultants to meet some of the aforementioned gaps. This study did not explore the SSAOs' satisfaction with the use of those external partners, nor did it ask SSAOs to rank the perceived effectiveness and value of using external partners. Further analysis is needed in this area.

Whatever a senior student affairs officer's reason for engaging in outcomes assessment and for using external partnerships, it seems clear that if outcomes assessment is not made an institutional priority, limited resources will always remain a reason to not conduct assessment (Palomba and Banta, 1999; Upcraft and Schuh, 1996). Can external partners help in this endeavor by making their tools and services affordable to every type of institution? Can institutions afford not to engage in external partnerships in order to make their outcomes assessment systematic and continuous?

Palomba and Banta (1999) and Upcraft and Schuh (1996) would argue that it would be short-sighted for student affairs professionals to disregard outcomes assessment. It may be to each institution's benefit to decide exactly what the intended development and learning outcomes are for each of its programs, draft an assessment plan, and then form internal and external partnerships to address those needs. Answers to each institution's assessment challenges are discernable. Some of these answers are available through the formation of a partnership with external vendors. Some of the solutions may take time to resolve as institutions work to articulate what is of meaning to them so that they can then assess it (Maki, 2002; Palomba and Banta, 1999). However, an institution must begin to improve its outcomes assessment efforts somewhere, and an excellent first step is to weigh internal tools and talent against what is available in the external marketplace. One may find inspiration and resolution in those places, or conversely, more questions in need of answers.

### References

American College Personnel Association (ACPA)'s Commission IX. Assessment for Student Development Clearinghouse. Washington D.C.: ACPA, 1999. [http://www.acpa.nche.edu/comms/comm09/dragon/dragon-index.html].

American College Testing (ACT) Postsecondary Services. Student Opinion Survey. Iowa City, Iowa: ACT, 1997.

Anderson, J. A. "Why Assessment Is Important to Student Affairs." *NASPA NetResults E-Zine,* Aug. 7, 2001, pp. 1–3. [http://www.naspa.org/netresults/index.cfm].

Baker, R. W., and Siryk, B. *Student Adaptation to College Questionnaire.* Los Angeles: Western Psychological Services, 1989.

Banta, T. W., Black, K. E., and Kline, K. A. "The Challenge to Assess Outcomes in Student Affairs." *NASPA NetResults E-Zine,* Aug. 28, 2001, pp. 1–6. [http://www.naspa.org/netresults/index.cfm].

Baxter-Magdola, M. B., and Porterfield, W. D. Measure of Epistemological Reflection. Oxford, Ohio: Miami University, 1985.

Borden, V.M.H., and Zak Owens, J. L. *Measuring Quality: Choosing Among Surveys and Other Assessments of College Quality.* Washington D.C.: American Council on Education Center for Policy Analysis and the Association for Institutional Research, 2001.

Brown, K. "Why Aren't Faculty Jumping on the Assessment Bandwagon—and What Can be Done to Encourage Their Involvement?" *Assessment Update, 13*(2), Apr.-May 2001, pp. 8–9, 16.

Cooperative Institutional Research Program. Los Angeles: University of California–Los Angeles, 2001. [http://www.collegeboard.com].

Educational Testing Services. Princeton, N.J., 2001. [http://www.ets.org].

Ennis, R. H., and Millman, J. "Cornell Critical Thinking Test." N.Y.: Cornell Critical Thinking Project, 1964.

Facione, P.A., and Facione, N.C. California Critical Thinking Dispositions Inventory. Millbrae, Calif.: California Academic Press, 1992.

Facione, P.A. and Facione, N.C. California Critical Thinking Skills Test. Millbrae, Calif.: California Academic Press, 1998.

Fultz, M. L., and Wong, L. E. "Creating and Sustaining an Assessment Culture." *Assessment Update, 2*(13), Apr.-May, 2001, pp. 12–13.

Gibbs, J. C., and Widaman, K. F. "Social Reflection Questionnaire." Columbus, Ohio: Ohio State University, 1982.

Gordon, V. N., and Habley, W. R. *Academic Advising: A Comprehensive Handbook.* San Francisco: Jossey-Bass, 2000.

Helm, K. "Minutes from the Committee on Undergraduate Academic Program Review." North Carolina State University, 2001. [http://www.ncsu.edu/provost/governance/Ad_hoc/CUPR].

Heppner, P. P. *The Problem Solving Inventory Manual.* Palo Alto, Calif.: Consulting Psychologists Press, 1988.

Higher Education Research Institute—UCLA Graduate School of Education and Information Studies. "Your First College Year." Los Angeles: HERI, 2001.

Interact Communications. "Student Satisfaction Surveys and Focus Groups." Onalaska, Wis.: Interact, 2001. [http://www.interactcom.com/crmrsss.html].

Knefelkamp, L. L., and Widick, C. "Measure of Intellectual Development." New York: Center for the Study of Intellectual Development, 1974.

Maki, P. "Using Multiple Assessment Methods to Explore Student Learning and Development Inside and Outside of the Classroom." *NASPA NetResults E-Zine,* Jan. 15, 2002, pp. 1–4. [http://www.naspa.org/netresults/index.cfm].

National Survey of Student Engagement. "College Student Report." Bloomington, Ind.: NSSE, 2001.

Noel-Levitz Centers. "Student Satisfaction Inventory." Iowa City, Iowa: Noel-Levitz, 2001.

North Carolina State University. University Planning and Analysis Assessment Resources Website. Raleigh, N.C.: North Carolina State University, 2001. [http://www2.acs.ncsu.edu/UPA/assmt/resource.htm].

North Carolina State University Committee on Undergraduate Academic Program Review. "Guidelines for Undergraduate Academic Program Review." Raleigh, N.C.: North Carolina State University, 2001. [http://www.ncsu.edu/provost/academic_programs/uapr/UAPRindx.html].

Palomba, G. D., and Banta, T. W. *Assessment Essentials: Planning, Implementing, and Improving Assessment in Higher Education.* San Francisco: Jossey-Bass, 1999.

Rest, J. "Defining Issues Test." Minneapolis, Minn.: University of Minnesota, 1979.

Rosenberg, M. *Society and the Adolescent Self-Image.* Princeton, N.J.: Princeton University Press, 1965.

Schuh, J. H., and Upcraft, M. L. "Assessment in Student Affairs: Let's Get Started." *NASPA NetResults E-Zine,* Dec. 4, 2001, pp. 1–4. [http://www.naspa.org/netresults/index.cfm].

Southern Association of Colleges and Schools. "Guidelines for Accreditation," 2001. [http://www.sacscog.org].

Super, D. E., and others. "Career Development Inventory." Palo Alto, Calif.: Consulting Psychologists Press, 1981.

Upcraft, M. L., and Schuh, J. H. *Assessment in Student Affairs: A Guide for Practitioners.* San Francisco: Jossey-Bass, 1996.

Watson, G., and Glaser, E. *Critical Thinking Appraisal.* San Antonio, TX: The Psychological Corporation, 1980.

Weinstein, C. E., Palmer, D. R., and Schulte, A. C. *Learning and Study Strategies Inventory.* Clearwater, Fla.: H&H Publishing, 1987.

*MARILEE J. BRESCIANI is the director of assessment for the division of undergraduate affairs and a visiting assistant professor in the College of Education at North Carolina State University.*

# INDEX

# Back Issue/Subscription Order Form

Copy or detach and send to:

**Jossey-Bass, A Wiley Company, 989 Market Street, San Francisco CA 94103-1741**

**Call or fax toll-free: Phone 888-378-2537 6:30AM – 3PM PST; Fax 888-481-2665**

Back Issues: Please send me the following issues at $27 each
(Important: please include ISBN number with your order.)

_____

_____

_____

$ _____ Total for single issues

$ _____ SHIPPING CHARGES: SURFACE    Domestic Canadian

| | | Domestic | Canadian |
|---|---|---|---|
| First Item | | $5.00 | $6.00 |
| Each Add'l Item | | $3.00 | $1.50 |

For next-day and second-day delivery rates, call the number listed above.

Subscriptions   Please __ start __ renew my subscription to *New Directions for Student Services* for the year 2_____ at the following rate:

| | | | |
|---|---|---|---|
| U.S. | __ Individual $70 | | __ Institutional $145 |
| Canada | __ Individual $70 | | __ Institutional $185 |
| All Others | __ Individual $94 | | __ Institutional $219 |
| Online Subscription | | | __ Institutional $145 |

**For more information about online subscriptions visit
www.interscience.wiley.com**

$ _____ Total single issues and subscriptions (Add appropriate sales tax for your state for single issue orders. No sales tax for U.S. subscriptions. Canadian residents, add GST for subscriptions and single issues.)

__Payment enclosed (U.S. check or money order only)
__VISA __ MC __ AmEx __ Discover Card #_____ Exp. Date _____

Signature _____ Day Phone _____
__Bill Me (U.S. institutional orders only. Purchase order required.)

Purchase order # _____
Federal Tax ID13559302          GST 89102 8052

Name _____

Address _____

_____

Phone _____ E-mail _____

For more information about Jossey-Bass, visit our Web site at www.josseybass.com

**PROMOTION CODE ND03**

SS95    The Implications of Student Spirituality for Student Affairs Practice
        *Margaret A. Jablonski*
        Provides student affairs professionals and others on college campuses with
        information and guidance about including spirituality in student life
        programs and in the curriculum of preparation programs. Explores the role
        that faith and spirit play in individual and group development on our
        campuses. Models of leadership, staff development, and graduate education
        itself are all examined from the context of spirituality.
        ISBN: 0-7879-5787-9

SS94    Consumers, Adversaries, and Partners: Working with the Families of
        Undergraduates
        *Bonnie V. Daniel, B. Ross Scott*
        Presents effective strategies for student services professionals to collaborate
        and coordinate in creating a consistent message of engagement for the
        families of today's college students. Parents, stepparents, grandparents, and
        others who serve as guardians of college students are challenging
        administrators to address their concerns in a variety of areas, including
        admissions and financial aid processes, orientation programs, residence life,
        and alumni and development activities.
        ISBN: 0-7879-5786-0

SS93    Student Services for Athletes
        *Mary F. Howard-Hamilton, Sherry K. Watt*
        Explores a full range of issues, including the ongoing impact of Title IX, the
        integration of student athletes into on-campus residence halls, the college
        experience for minority athletes, and the expansion of opportunities for
        women athletes.
        ISBN: 0-7879-5757-7

SS92    Leadership and Management Issues for a New Century
        *Dudley B. Woodard Jr., Patrick Love, Susan R. Komives*
        Examines new approaches to learning requiring a new kind of leadership,
        and describes the important role played by student affairs professionals in
        creating and sustaining learning communities. Explores how changes in
        students will affect student affairs work, outlines new dimensions of student
        affairs capital, and details the importance of active and collaborative
        leadership for creating a more flexible structure to handle future challenges.
        ISBN: 0-7879-5445-4

SS91    Serving Students with Disabilities
        *Holley A. Belch*
        Explores the critical role that community and dignity play in creating a
        meaningful educational experience for students with disabilities and shows
        how to help these students gain meaningful access and full participation in
        campus activities. Addresses such common concerns as fulfilling legal
        requirements and overcoming architectural barriers, as well as effective
        approaches to recruitment and retention, strategies for career and academic
        advising, and the impact of financial resources on funding programs and
        services.
        ISBN: 0-7879-5444-6

SS90    **Powerful Programming for Student Learning: Approaches That Make a
        Difference**
        *Debora L. Liddell, Jon P. Lund*
        Assists student affairs professionals as they plan, implement, and evaluate
        their educational interventions on college and university campuses. Details
        each step of program assessment, planning, implementation, and outcome
        evaluation. Explains the importance of collaborating with faculty and others,
        illustrating several types of programming partnerships with four brief case
        studies, and examines the significant partnership aspects that led to
        programming success.
        ISBN: 0-7879-5443-8


SS89    **The Role Student Aid Plays in Enrollment Management**
        *Michael D. Coomes*
        Discusses the political and cultural contexts that influence decisions about
        student aid and enrollment management, the special enrollment
        management challenges facing independent colleges, and some alternative
        methods for financing a college education. Provides a review of the research
        on the impact of student aid on recruitment and retention,
        recommendations for ethical enrollment planning, and a list of resources for
        enrollment planners, researchers, and policymakers.
        ISBN: 0-7879-5378-4


SS88    **Understanding and Applying Cognitive Development Theory**
        *Patrick G. Love, Victoria L. Guthrie*
        Reviews five theories of the cognitive development of college students and
        explores the applications of those theories for student affairs practice. These
        theories shed light on gender-related patterns of knowing and reasoning;
        interpersonal, cultural, and emotional influences on cognitive development;
        and people's methods of approaching complex issues and defending what
        they believe.
        ISBN: 0-7879-4870-5


SS87    **Creating Successful Partnerships Between Academic and Student Affairs**
        *John H. Schuh, Elizabeth J. Whitt*
        Presents case studies of academic and student affairs partnerships that have
        been successfully put into practice at a variety of institutions, in areas such
        as service learning, the core curriculum, and residential learning
        communities.
        ISBN: 0-7879-4869-1


SS86    **Beyond Borders: How International Developments Are Changing
        International Affairs Practice**
        *Diane L. Cooper, James M. Lancaster*
        Assesses the impact of international trends and developments on the student
        affairs profession and offers practical suggestions for developing the
        knowledge and skills requisite for a global future. Explains how to recruit
        and support international students and provide valuable information on
        student and staff exchange programs. Presents case studies from student
        affairs professionals in Mexico, Germany, and Hong Kong, highlighting the
        global student affairs issues that transcend national borders.
        ISBN: 0-7879-4868-3

**SS85**  **Student Affairs Research, Evaluation, and Assessment: Structure and Practice in an Era of Change**
*Gary D. Malaney*
Describes how student affairs and faculty can collaborate to create an agenda for student-related research; reviews technological aids for collecting and analyzing data; and discusses how student affairs researchers can make their role more vital to the campus by expanding into policy analysis and information brokering.
ISBN: 0-7879-4216-2

**SS84**  **Strategies for Staff Development: Personal and Professional Education in the 21st Century**
*William A. Bryan, Robert A. Schwartz*
Offers a range of strategies for recruiting, retaining, and developing an educated, energetic, and motivated student affairs staff. Examines a performance-based approach to human resource development, the impact of supervisors and mentors on those entering and advancing in the field, and the influence of behavioral style on professional development.
ISBN: 0-7879-4455-6

**SS83**  **Responding to the New Affirmative Action Climate**
*Donald D. Gehring*
Explores how to achieve an economically, ethnically, spiritually, and culturally diverse student body while complying with confusing and sometimes conflicting laws and judicial pronouncements. Clarifies the law as it relates to affirmative action in admissions and financial aid; discusses alternatives to race-based methods for achieving diversity; and reports on a national study of student affairs programs that have successfully used affirmative action.
ISBN: 0-7879-4215-4

**SS82**  **Beyond Law and Policy: Reaffirming the Role of Student Affairs**
*Diane L. Cooper, James M. Lancaster*
Examines higher education's apparent over-reliance on policy and shows how we can redirect our attention to the ethical and developmental issues that underlie the undergraduate experience. Discusses how learning communities and creeds can help achieve balance between policy and personal responsibility; how to deal with student misconduct in a way that both reduces the risk of litigation and furthers student development; and how to promote multiculturalism without compromising individual rights and freedoms.
ISBN: 0-7879-4214-6

**SS80**  **Helping African American Men Succeed in College**
*Michael J. Cuyjet*
Offers practical strategies, proven models and programs, and the essential theoretical grounding necessary for nurturing and retaining African American male students. Explores ways to make classroom environments more supportive; the benefits of mentoring initiatives; the opportunities for leadership development on a predominantly white campus; and more.
ISBN: 0-7879-9883-4

## NEW DIRECTIONS FOR STUDENT SERVICES IS NOW AVAILABLE ONLINE AT WILEY INTERSCIENCE

### What is Wiley InterScience?

*Wiley InterScience* is the dynamic online content service from John Wiley & Sons delivering the full text of over 300 leading scientific, technical, medical, and professional journals, plus major reference works, the acclaimed *Current Protocols* laboratory manuals, and even the full text of select Wiley print books online.

### What are some special features of Wiley InterScience?

*Wiley InterScience Alerts* is a service that delivers table of contents via e-mail for any journal available on Wiley InterScience as soon as a new issue is published online.
*Early View* is Wiley's exclusive service presenting individual articles online as soon as they are ready, even before the release of the compiled print issue. These articles are complete, peer-reviewed, and citable.
*CrossRef* is the innovative multi-publisher reference linking system enabling readers to move seamlessly from a reference in a journal article to the cited publication, typically located on a different server and published by a different publisher.

### How can I access Wiley InterScience?

Visit http://www.interscience.wiley.com

*Guest Users* can browse Wiley InterScience for unrestricted access to journal Tables of Contents and Article Abstracts, or use the powerful search engine.
*Registered Users* are provided with a *Personal Home Page* to store and manage customized alerts, searches, and links to favorite journals and articles. Additionally, Registered Users can view free Online Sample Issues and preview selected material from major reference works.
*Licensed Customers* are entitled to access full-text journal articles in PDF, with select journals also offering full-text HTML.

### How do I become an Authorized User?

*Authorized Users* are individuals authorized by a paying Customer to have access to the journals in Wiley InterScience. For example, a university that subscribes to Wiley journals is considered to be the Customer. Faculty, staff and students authorized by the university to have access to those journals in Wiley InterScience are Authorized Users. Users should contact their Library for information on which Wiley journals they have access to in Wiley InterScience.

## ASK YOUR INSTITUTION ABOUT WILEY INTERSCIENCE TODAY!